Birmingham

THEN AND NOW

Birmingham

THEN AND NOW

Alan Clawley

BATSFORD

First published in the United Kingdom in 2013 by
Batsford
10 Southcombe Street
London
W14 0RA

An imprint of Anova Books Company Ltd

Copyright © Anova Books 2013

The moral rights of the author have been asserted

ISBN: 978-1-84994-021-4

A CIP catalogue record for this book is available from the British Library.

18 17 16 15 14 13
10 9 8 7 6 5 4 3 2 1

Reproduction by Rival Colour Ltd, UK
Printed by 1010 Printing International Ltd, China

This book can be ordered direct from the publisher at the website: www.anovabooks.com

Front and back covers show: New Street, 1890 (Mary Evans Picture Library) and now (Aidan O'Rourke).

Pages 1 and 2 show: Chamberlain Square, c. 1900 (Getty Images) and now (Aidan O'Rourke).

AUTHOR'S ACKNOWLEDGEMENTS
My special thanks to David Salmo for his enthusiasm for Birmingham and his unwavering support for the book and its author. I was pleased to work with Aidan O'Rourke, whose splendid photographs are in the book and to meet up with him on his visits to Birmingham; Urban Splash kindly gave permission for Aidan to take the photographs from a penthouse balcony on the top of the Rotunda. The Local Studies Department of Birmingham Central Library was invaluable for its open access to historic maps, local history books and street directories. The staff of the University of Birmingham and King Edward's Grammar School were most helpful in providing archive photos whilst Mark Norton kindly gave permission to include one from his father's archive.

My wife Hazel was always willing to help me when a picture was still an unsolved puzzle or to suggest when a caption was less than clear and needed to be changed. Apologies to those friends, colleagues and archivists who suggested subjects or helped track down old photos but which for various reasons did not make it into the book. *Birmingham Then and Now* is dedicated to my grandchildren Ruby and Alex who will inherit the Birmingham we leave behind.

The worldwide web has become an instantaneous source of information with many sites specialising in the social and topographical history of local areas, topics like transport, and industries that have now almost disappeared from the real world, but there are still lots of books, trail guides, and historic maps of Birmingham. Those I used most in the preparation of the book are listed below and are recommended.

Books
Buteaux, Simon, *Beneath the Bull Ring: The Archaeology of Life and Death in Early Birmingham* (2003)
Clawley, Alan, *John Madin: Twentieth Century Architects* (2011)
Foster, Andy, *Birmingham: Pevsner Architectural Guides* (2005)
Hill, Rosemary, *God's Architect: Pugin and the Building of Romantic Britain* (2007)
Hodder, Michael, *Birmingham, The Hidden History* (2004)
Pevsner, Nikolaus and Wedgwood, Alexandra, *Warwickshire: The Buildings of England* (1966)
Skipp, Victor, *The Making of Victorian Birmingham* (1983)

Trail Guides
Pugin Society, *The Birmingham Pugin Trail*
Birmingham City Council, *Matthew Boulton City Centre Walk* and *Birmingham Jewellery Quarter Heritage Trail*

Maps
Alan Godfrey Maps, *Central Birmingham 1902–11* (2010)
British History Online, *Ordnance Survey 1890*

PHOTO CREDITS
The publisher wishes to thank the following for kindly providing photographs for this book:

All 'Then' photographs are from Anova Image Library, except for the following: Getty Images: 1, 6, 12 main, 16 inset, 18, 22, 28, 32, 34, 36 main, 52 main, 56 main, 62, 68, 80 main, 86, 90, 92, 96, 120, 122, 126, 128, 134. Phyllis Nicklin Collection, University of Birmingham: 24, 42 main, 50, 54, 56 inset, 70, 72 main, 74, 76, 80 inset, 84, 88, 94, 110, 130, 142. Mirrorpix: 47 inset, 48, 118, 136, 138. Alamy: 78, 98, 99, 106 main, 113. Mary Evans Picture Library: 10, 30. English Heritage: 44, 104. King Edward's Foundation Archive: 8. English Heritage (Aerofilms Collection): 112. Mark Norton: 132. Richard Postill: 46. Corbis: 38.

All 'Now' photographs are by Aidan O'Rourke, except for the following: Alan Clawley: 23 inset, 75, 89. Oosoom: 41 inset. Neil (Football Rambles): 93. Urbansplash: 105 inset. Steve Cadman: 127 inset.

Introduction

For those who enjoy solving puzzles and working out how things have changed, Birmingham is a treasure house. One could spend days on just one street fathoming out which old buildings have gone. But for architecture enthusiasts or lovers of the past, Birmingham can be frustrating and at times depressing. Parts of the city have undergone complete redevelopment more than once in living memory.

The Romans marched through Birmingham on Icknield Street and built a fort where University Station stands today, but their presence seems unrelated to the settlement at Digbeth. Nothing remains there of the 'ham' settled by the Anglo-Saxon Beorma and his followers or 'ingas'. The Domesday Book records that in 1086 the Norman lord Richard 'held four hides' in Birmingham. By the 12th century Birmingham had a moated manor house where the Wholesale Market now stands, a parish church, a market place, forerunner of the Bullring, rows of wooden houses and a deer park.

From its medieval core, the town expanded in the 18th century on higher ground to the north, beginning with Old Square. But it was in the Victorian era, particularly under the mayoralty of Joseph Chamberlain, that Birmingham became the vast industrial city that we are left with today. Since it became a borough in 1838, Birmingham has had to keep extending its boundaries to house a population that rose from 70,000 to one million. At first only Deritend, Bordesley, Duddeston, Nechells and Edgbaston were included, but by 1891 the old villages of Balsall Heath, Harborne, Saltley and Little Bromwich were swallowed up, followed by Aston, Sheldon, Yardley, Kings Norton, Northfield, Quinton and Handsworth.

Despite its habit of sweeping away much of the evidence, Birmingham has a rich history. It played a crucial role in the Industrial Revolution, was birthplace of several famous banks, city of a thousand trades and pioneer of municipal socialism. The city was also a hotbed of invention and engineering – it produced the world's first transverse-engine mini-car and the Spitfire aeroplane, and it built more canals than Venice. Other innovations include Spaghetti Junction, the earliest purpose-built cinema, the first new Roman Catholic Cathedral since the Reformation and the world's first mainline railway station.

There is so much history that Birmingham folk can hardly be blamed for being a bit blasé about it and not valuing it as much as they should. Birmingham doesn't dwell on its past: as the Corporation's motto 'Forward' indicates, it gets most excited about the new. Its factories and its products come and go with the ebb and flow of fashion. The car factories of Longbridge have disappeared with hardly a murmur from the huge army of workers who once populated their production lines.

Some buildings, streets and squares in Birmingham have become a permanent feature of the city and labelled as 'heritage' that is not for sale. Even in a city that loves novelty and change there is clearly a need to keep something of the past. This can be in the form of complete buildings like the Town Hall or public parks like Cannon Hill, the futures of which are now more or less secure. Other examples in the book are the Old Crown Inn, the School of Art, the Victoria Law Courts and the modern Rotunda.

We rather take it for granted that city churches and cathedrals will be with us forever, but the demolition of Christ Church should remind us of their vulnerability in the commercial heart of the city. Some lost buildings are only commemorated by a piece of public art on the site where an important building like the Lucas factory once stood. Even architectural gems like King Edward's Grammar School in New Street may only be marked by a blue plaque on the building that replaced it. The only physical remains of the demolished Victorian Central Reference Library building are a cast-iron spiral staircase and the wood-panelled Shakespeare Room, which has already been passed on like a family heirloom to a new home in the Library of Birmingham in Centenary Square.

The fate of some parts of the city seems to be that of continual change, crucibles in which the latest fashion in architecture, shopping centres or civic centres are reinvented. Perhaps this character trait is rooted in the historic 'toy' or small metal goods trade and the sale of cheap disposable novelties, which was carried into the 20th century by the car industry. The Bullring is the prime architectural example but Paradise Circus and Corporation Street are next on the list for dramatic change. As a result, not only do visitors to Birmingham find it hard to navigate the city, but people born and bred here have come to accept that they can never be entirely familiar with their own city centre.

The examples in this book illustrate yet another contradiction in the city's character: mass production versus arts and crafts. Although the jewellery trade is a hand-craft industry based in small workshops in the Jewellery Quarter, it also produced on a mass scale. Perhaps it is not surprising that the city that gave birth to the Industrial Revolution should also have supported a reaction to it in the Romantic movements in art, architecture and music. Birmingham School of Art is the home of the Arts and Crafts movement, and the City Art Gallery houses a major collection of Pre-Raphaelite art. Longbridge is the ultimate example of mass production – the automated production line.

The number of subjects in the book on transport hints at the need for a midland city to find ways of exporting its manufactured goods and importing its raw materials. Birmingham was a pioneer in canal navigation and rail travel, with its early Curzon Street Station and two mainline railway stations built right in the centre of the city. It led the way in aviation too, with its municipal airport at Elmdon. It is of course most famous for Spaghetti Junction that connects the city centre with the national motorway network that passes through the city.

Other examples in the book show the philanthropic side of Birmingham's wealthy Victorians. Sir Josiah Mason's college of science became the great University of Birmingham, while George Cadbury left us Bournville, which still inspires town planners and social housing providers today.

Finally, the historic rivalry between Aston Villa FC and Birmingham City FC perhaps exemplifies the dual character of Birmingham – the one flying at the highest level the other modest and self-deprecating. Edgbaston is of course the home of the cricket club that represents the ancient county of Warwickshire to which Birmingham once belonged.

NEW STREET

One of Birmingham's oldest streets and the first to be pedestrianised

Left: The name New Street is misleading as it is one of the city's oldest thoroughfares. It was first mentioned as long ago as 1397, shortly after the Gild Hall of 1392 was built there before King Edward's Grammar School replaced it. Until the 17th century it comprised just a few cottages and barns, but by the middle of the 19th century it had become a fashionable shopping street. Traffic is still thin enough for a man to wander down the middle of New Street in this photo from the 1930s. The Town Hall closes off the view at the top end of the street, but the classical 1829 portico of the Society of Arts, which once projected into the street, was demolished in 1922. On the left is the entrance canopy of the Midland Hotel, where a young Mantovani was in charge of his own orchestra before launching his easy-listening recording career that made him 'Britain's most successful album act before the Beatles'. On the right is the upmarket men's clothes shop Austin Reed. Opened in 1913, it was the first Austin Reed outside of London.

Above: By the mid 1980s traffic in New Street had become intolerable. New Street's narrow pavements and choking traffic fumes made the case for Birmingham's first experiment in pedestrianisation and eventually all motor vehicles were banned except for deliveries. The kerbs were taken out and the whole area paved over in patterns of coloured brick. Mature trees were planted down the middle and benches installed. This was so successful that in 1997 the Birmingham Civic Society decided to award its annual Forward Prize to the City Planning Department for its work. New Street has now become the home for various street events throughout the year. A farmers' market visits every other Wednesday and in the run-up to Christmas it is thronged with visitors to the popular German Street Market. Every September the street hosts a row of stalls promoting the many cultural organisations taking part in the free Artsfest. A post-modern Council information kiosk now stands in New Street near Stephenson Place. The Midland Hotel is now occupied by the Burlington Hotel while Austin Reed has given way to another men's retailer, Ted Baker. The Town Hall still closes off the view at the top end of the street (see inset).

KING EDWARD'S GRAMMAR SCHOOL / KING EDWARD HOUSE

Barry and Pugin's neo-Gothic masterpiece was demolished in 1936

Left: Down a side alley on the south side of New Street, nearly opposite Union Passage, a blue plaque marks this as the site of the 'GILD HALL of HOLY CROSS 1392 and from 1552 to 1936 KING EDWARD VI SCHOOL'. The school building that stood here from 1836 until its demolition in 1936 was designed by Charles Barry with Augustus Welby Pugin in 1835. The two formed such a successful partnership that they were later appointed as architects and designers of the Palace of Westminster. Pugin's connection with Birmingham remained strong for the rest of his career. In 1838 he persuaded John Hardman junior (1811–67) to turn his Birmingham button-making business to making the metalwork and later stained glass for his new churches. Based in the Jewellery Quarter, the Hardman firm rose to fame as makers of fine medieval-style metalwork based on Pugin's research, drawings and publications.

Above: Today the Pugin Society celebrates his remaining work in a new guide entitled *The Birmingham Pugin Trail*. The demolition of the Grammar School in 1936 seems today like an act of wanton destruction that is impossible to imagine happening again. In its place is a commercial block, the King Edward Building, and the Odeon cinema, which opened as the Paramount in 1937. The school moved to a 50-acre site in Edgbaston, near the University, taking with it some Pugin-designed furniture as well as the entire upper corridor, which was dismantled stone by stone and rebuilt as a war memorial chapel in the new school. New Street was pedestrianised and planted with mature trees in the 1990s to remove the noise, smell and hazards of heavy traffic and to encourage street traders and buskers back to the street.

MIDLAND BANK / WATERSTONE'S BOOKSHOP

This exuberant symbol of Victorian self-confidence has been given new life as a bookshop

Left: The Midland Bank was one of two banks that Birmingham bequeathed to the modern world, the other being Lloyds. Founded in 1836 as the Birmingham and Midland Bank with its first premises in Union Street, the Midland Bank became a financial institution of national then international status. Its main head office was in New Street, a building designed like a palace by Edward Holmes between 1867 and 1869. The bank, with its grand Ionic columns, is on the left in this photo from 1890. Next to the bank, in Stephenson Place, is the statue of parliamentary reformer Thomas Attwood (1783–1856). Attwood was also a partner in Spooner and Attwood's Bank and argued that economic slumps from which the country was suffering could be avoided by the introduction of bank notes that were not exchangeable for gold.

Above: The takeover of the Midland Bank by the Hong Kong and Shanghai Banking Corporation (HSBC) in 1992 resulted in the closure of the New Street premises as a bank. A year later, the building was taken over by Waterstone's and turned into a bookshop under the supervision of the Malcolm Payne Design Group. This involved raising the central dome lantern by a full storey, but otherwise the opulent character of the original banking hall with its grand staircase was faithfully preserved and enhanced. The Attwood statue that stood in Stephenson Place was moved to Sparkbrook in 1974 but in 2008 it was placed in storage. There is however a new sculpture of him by Sioban Coppinger and Fiona Peever that depicts him reclining nonchalantly on the steps of Chamberlain Square by the Town Hall. It was commissioned by his great-great-grand-daughter Priscilla Mitchell in 1993. Since then its unusual ensemble of full-size figure, soap box and bronze 'papers' lying on the ground has made it a popular photo opportunity for visitors to the city.

NEW STREET STATION

The history of the city's central station illustrates the changing technology, ownership and style of train travel

Left: It seems odd that the main entrance to New Street Station was never in New Street itself. It was behind the station's Queen's Hotel building on Stephenson Street, shown here in 1962, where taxis could drop off their customers. From the start the platforms were 7m (25ft) below New Street, but a footbridge was provided across them from one side of the station to the other on the line of an old right of way. The station itself, which is hidden behind the hotel, was opened in 1852 when the train shed was the largest glass and iron roof in the world, with its span of 65m (212ft) and overall length of 330m (1,080ft). No doubt it was felt necessary to provide as much air and natural light as possible to dissipate the black smoke and sulphurous fumes of the steam engines when the c. 1910 inset photo was taken. In the 1950s the railways had been nationalised under British Railways who imposed a uniform house-style and typography on the historic railway regions and embarked on a programme of replacing steam locomotives with mainline diesel locomotives or multiple-unit diesel rail-cars.

Above: The view from the ramp that modern passengers follow up into the shopping centre above the station is very different without the imposing hotel building that so clearly marked the main pedestrian entrance to the station. As part of the West Coast Main Line modernisation programme, the old station and Queen's Hotel were demolished between 1964 and 1966. When the new station opened in 1967 the main entrance shifted to Worcester Street, where cars and taxis could pull in to drop off and pick up passengers. Instead of having platforms that were flooded in natural light from a vast glass roof, the platforms were now buried underneath the concrete floor of a shopping centre, since named The Pallasades. The need to derive financial return by building a shopping centre above the station was crucial and remains so today. Work is now in hand to revamp the station's 1960s architecture and to introduce natural light into the shopping centre by cutting a large skylight in the roof.

PARADISE STREET

The loss of two landmark buildings has transformed this view of Paradise Street

Left: In 1890, when this photo was taken, the solid-looking Christ Church closed the end of Paradise Street. In front of the portico is a statue of Sir Robert Peel (1788–1850), twice British prime minister. The church was opened in 1814 and its spire was much criticised because it replaced the cupola that was originally intended. New Street is not visible from here but leads off to the right of the church. The big building far left is the Birmingham and Midland Institute. The nearest section is John Henry Chamberlain's elaborate neo-gothic design of 1881 but the section that curves round the corner into Ratcliff Place was designed by Charles Barry in 1855–57 in the classical style. Alexander Munro's statue of James Watt made in 1868, guards the opening to Ratcliff Place which runs parallel to the long side of the Town Hall.

Above: Christ Church was demolished in 1899 and in its place a French Renaissance style office block known as Galloways Corner was built. This was in turn demolished in 1970 for a section of the Ring Road that was not built, and replaced by the block that can be seen in the photograph beyond the yellow banners in Victoria Square. Today Christ Church Passage still marks the boundary of the long gone church. The Birmingham and Midland Institute was demolished in the 1970s and now more of the side of Town Hall can be seen from Paradise Street. The ground on the left has been given over to vehicles that encircle the huge roundabout on the Ring Road known as Paradise Circus, on which the Central Library, Birmingham Conservatoire, Copthorne Hotel, Chamberlain House and Fletchers Walk await their turn for redevelopment. Both statues have been moved; Watt went to Chamberlain Square in front of the Central Library and Peel went to the Police Training College in Edgbaston.

TOWN HALL

Where Mendelssohn premiered his oratorio *Elijah* in 1846

Left: The Town Hall in Birmingham is not the centre of municipal administration as it is in most other towns and cities, but a public concert hall. Modelled on the temple of Castor and Pollux in the Roman Forum, it has a facade of fluted Corinthian columns resting on a high rusticated podium built in brick and faced with Anglesey marble. The council chamber and offices were housed later in the Council House, the clock tower of which peeps over the Town Hall roof on the left. The Town Hall seen here in the 1920s from Ratcliff Place, was opened in 1834 and extended in 1837 to provide a worthy venue for the Triennial Music Festival. It was paid for by donations and public subscriptions and built to the designs of Hansom and Welch. The first performance of Mendelssohn's oratorio *Elijah* was conducted here by the composer himself and sung by the newly created Birmingham Festival Choral Society in 1846. Charles Dickens read excerpts from *A Christmas Carol* here in 1853. The statue in front of the Town Hall is of theologian and scientist Joseph Priestley (1733–1804), who discovered oxygen in 1774. The inset photo shows the concert pipe organ by William Hill that was installed in 1834.

Above: By the mid 1990s the building was in a poor state of repair and was closed to the public. After lying empty for years, a sum of £35 million was raised from the Heritage Lottery Fund, European Regional Development Fund and City Council to completely refurbish the building inside and out. It was re-opened in October 2007 and in April 2008 the Birmingham Festival Choral Society once again performed *Elijah* to a capacity audience. The outside of the building is just the same as when it was built, but inside the gallery was restored to its original shape and the acoustics improved by the installation of clear speaker baffles suspended below the ornate ceiling. Now branded TH, the venue is owned and managed by a new charitable body that also owns the Symphony Hall. The statue of Priestley was eventually placed at the front of the Central Library when Chamberlain Place was refurbished during the late 1980s. The spot where the statue stood is now part of Paradise Circus Queensway.

VICTORIA SQUARE

Council House Square was renamed Victoria Square after the death of the monarch in 1901

Left: The Council House, which dominates this view of Victoria Square, is the city's most important civic building. The full council, presently of 120 members, meets here in a semi-circular chamber. It was built in 1870–79 to the classical design of Yeoville Thomason. The main photo was taken in 1962 when Queen Victoria stood on a traffic island and was the only statue left in the square. Although there is only one black cab in sight, it is clear from the 'NO ENTRY' and 'NO WAITING' signs that the traffic management scheme that made the city centre infamous was well under way. The inset picture of the Victory Parade at the end of the Second World War shows that the square was then the city's most important place for big public assemblies, a role once intended for the much bigger parade ground on Broad Street that had not yet been completed. The white marble statue of Queen Victoria (died 1901) by Thomas Brock is accompanied by that of Edward VII (died 1910) by Albert Toft in this photo from 1945.

Above: The Council House today is not blackened by sooty air. Nowadays Victoria Square gets filled with the German Market in what looks like being an annual build-up to Christmas. The space has been given over to pedestrians and is now occupied by a set of sculptures and fountains designed by Dhruva Mistry that were opened by Princess Diana in 1994. The reclining nude in the top pool has been unofficially christened 'The Floozie in the Jacuzzi' (see inset). Queen Victoria's statue remains but was recast in bronze in 1951. The statue of Edward VII was moved to Highgate Park in 1951 but was restored and brought back to the city centre in 2010. It now stands in front of Baskerville House in Centenary Square.

CORBETT'S TEMPERANCE HOTEL / VICTORIA SQUARE HOUSE

The temperance hotel has been replaced by the sober General Post Office

Left: Corbett's Temperance Hotel is the main feature in this 1887 photograph from Victoria Square. Total abstinence was promoted by the temperance movement founded in Preston in 1832 by Joseph Livesey who lobbied unsuccessfully for many years for the total prohibition of alcohol. His intention was to counter the reputation working people had gained for drunkenness. He opened the first temperance hotel in 1833. The block which is dominated by the Corbett's Hotel is between Hill Street, going down steeply on the right, and Pinfold Street, partly hidden on the left in front of Draycott the Photographer. Paradise Street is to the right.

Above: The whole block, including Corbett's, between Hill Street and Pinfold Street was demolished and replaced by a new General Post Office designed by Sir Henry Tanner of the Office of Works in 1891. It is now named Victoria Square House. It was saved from demolition in 1974 following a campaign led by Friends of the Earth and the Victorian Society. The building that was occupied by Draycott the Photographer is still there in 2012 but the sign has been replaced by a window. The temporary wooden building in the foreground was erected for one of the many events that are held in the square throughout the year. Anthony Gormley's 'Iron Man', which leans at a jaunty angle, is partly visible on the other side of the temporary hut.

CHAMBERLAIN SQUARE

Joseph Chamberlain was honoured in his lifetime with this durable public fountain

Left: This c. 1900 view looks north to the neo-Gothic Joseph Chamberlain Memorial Fountain and the Council House clock tower that houses the Big Brum bell. The portico to the immediate right of the tower is the main entrance to the Museum and Art Gallery. The rusticated limestone base of the Town Hall and one of its columns is just coming into frame at the right edge of the photograph. The Chamberlain Memorial was unveiled in 1880 when Chamberlain was still only 44 years old. It was the work of architect J. H. Chamberlain (no relation) and was similar in style to the Albert Memorial in London, but with a fountain and round pool added. The building on the left is part of Josiah Mason's College, which became the University of Birmingham. A marble figure made by F. G. Williamson in 1885 of Mason sitting with his back to the college that bore his name can just be made out in the shade on the left of the picture. The smaller neo-Gothic canopy to the right of the fountain houses the statue of George Dawson, a nonconformist minister and contemporary of Joseph Chamberlain.

Above: The council buildings are unchanged, except for the temporary brightly coloured woollen stockings covering the columns of the Museum and Art Gallery. The Chamberlain Memorial has been fully restored and now sits approximately where it was before. Mason College was demolished in the 1960s. The Council House extension, with its connecting arched bridge over Edmund Street, was completed in 1917 and appears to the left of the clock tower. After being here for 65 years, Josiah Mason's statue was removed from the square. A bronze bust made from a restored head and shoulders now stands in the middle of a traffic roundabout on the Chester Road in Erdington, near the site of the Josiah Mason Orphanage. Summer flower boxes decorate the curved concrete facade of the 1974 Central Library to the left of the Chamberlain Memorial. The inverted ziggurat design of the library is shown inset, with the reclining statue of parliamentary reformer Thomas Attwood in the foreground.

CENTRAL REFERENCE LIBRARY / PARADISE CIRCUS QUEENSWAY

The loss of the old library for the city's inner ring road is still mourned by many today

Left: This 1968 photograph shows the deep excavation of the red sandstone of Birmingham's central ridge that was being dug for the Inner Ring Road to get from Suffolk Street to Great Charles Street. Over the tunnel the surface-level Paradise Circus Queensway and the foundations for the new Central Library, School of Music and shopping mall would be constructed. The building with the rounded end is the Central Reference Library. It was designed in the Italianate style by E. M. Barry and carried out by Martin & Chamberlain in 1863–65. It was restored after a fire in 1879 by J. H. Chamberlain, who also designed the extension on the right which Pevsner describes as a 'charming facade in the Lombardic Renaissance style of South Kensington, with plentiful mosaic and terracotta'. The Town Hall, the Council House and the Chamberlain Memorial can be seen on the left in Chamberlain Square.

Above: The Reference Library was demolished soon after the 1968 photo was taken and a concrete platform was built over Paradise Circus Queensway to provide a traffic-free precinct for pedestrians around and through the new Central Library. Today the semicircular amphitheatre with the Chamberlain Fountain at its centre is a popular outdoor venue for music events or just for sitting down. The new library, designed by local architect John Madin in the form of an inverted ziggurat, was opened by Harold Wilson in 1974. The photo is taken standing at the corner of the library on the bridge looking past the statue of James Watt that had been re-located from Ratcliff Place. Although these dramatic changes were only completed in the 1980s, there are already plans to demolish all the buildings on the Paradise Circus island (Central Library, Birmingham Conservatoire, Copthorne Hotel, Chamberlain House and Fletchers Walk) and replace them with commercial properties.

ANN STREET / COLMORE ROW

This old street in the city centre was straightened out and is now a Conservation Area

Left: The demise of Ann Street, shown here in 1867, was imminent judging by the appearance of the derelict building plastered with bill posters on the right. The 120-year leases granted by Ann Colmore in 1746, which allowed the development of the north (right-hand) side of the street named after her, had just expired. The buildings therefore date from the mid-18th century. The south (left-hand) side of the street was part of the Inge estate that was developed from 1823. When this photo was taken Joseph Chamberlain's vision for a grand new Council House and public square at the end of Ann Street would have already been on the drawing board. Ann Street is seen curving gently left to pass the south end of the 33-year-old Town Hall (the ghostly outline of which can just be seen), to reach the top end of New Street and Paradise Street.

Above: All the buildings in Ann Street were demolished in the 1870s to make a straight street leading to the front of the new Council House. Ann Street became what is now the section of Colmore Row between Newhall Street and Victoria Square. The City Council made the street a Conservation Area in 1971 to protect the buildings and townscape that existed at that date. The buildings on the south (left-hand) side date from 1875 to 1926 and were meant originally for various insurance companies including Atlas, Eagle and North British & Mercantile. The brownish building in sunlight is the former Eagle Insurance building of 1900, designed by W. R. Lethaby & J. L. Ball. It remains as an important example of Arts and Crafts Free Style architecture. Nearest the camera on the right-hand side of the street are three bollards at the entrance to a precinct that formed part of John Madin's 1974 NatWest Centre, a feature reminiscent of the Economist building in London. Just beyond is Seymour Harris's design in Portland stone that replaced part of the NatWest complex in 1997. The Town Hall remains the only constant in both photographs.

SNOW HILL STATION

Rising land values and the Beeching cuts resulted in the demise of Snow Hill's Victorian edifice

Left: With their monumental glass-roofed train sheds and opulent hotel frontages, the major Victorian railway stations added grandeur and presence to city views. Snow Hill, shown here c. 1900, is no exception. Snow Hill's Great Western Hotel on Colmore Row, was built over the tunnel from Moor Street and designed in the Classical style by W. G. Owen in 1852. Its corner turrets and prominent chimney stacks give it a castle-like appearance. The main entrance to the train sheds, which can be seen behind the building, is on Colmore Row, but the platforms were a long flight of steps below street level. Easier access to the trains was possible from Livery Street (on the left), which slopes steeply down to the same level as the platforms.

Above: The station building and the iron train shed were all demolished in 1977 to make way for the modern office development and multi-storey car park that occupy the site above ground level today. The tunnel to Moor Street was also closed but, with the help of grants from the European Regional Development Fund, it was re-opened. The station was rebuilt and opened for local services in 1987. In 1995 John Prescott MP came to Snow Hill to open the re-branded and enhanced 'Jewellery Line' from Snow Hill to Smethwick Galton Bridge. Along with the refurbishment of Moor Street Station and the upgrading of the Oxford line, there is now a direct rail service from Snow Hill to Paddington, and Worcester and Stratford upon Avon are also connected through the modern Snow Hill Station. Snow Hill is also the terminus of the Metro that runs to Wolverhampton and which is to be extended to New Street.

ST PHILIP'S CATHEDRAL

This former parish church was a worthy candidate to become the cathedral for the rapidly expanding diocese of Birmingham

Left: When this photo was taken this outstanding English Baroque building had only recently been adopted as the Cathedral Church of St Phillip. The Diocese of Birmingham was created in 1905 to cater for the rapid growth in the city's population. Originally it was a parish church designed by Thomas Archer, a pupil of Christopher Wren, built between 1709 and 1725 on a field then known as Horse Close. Its east end was extended by J. A. Chatwin in 1883–84. The churchyard was originally laid out with avenues of lime trees. The obelisk on the left was erected in 1885 to commemorate Colonel Burnaby who served in the army and died during the Sudan campaign of 1875. The stained glass in the west window is by Edward Burne-Jones who was born in 1833 nearby in Bennetts Hill. Morris & Co carried out the work in 1897 to Burne-Jones's designs. The windows depict the Ascension, the Nativity and the Annunciation to the Shepherds.

Above: The exterior appearance of the church itself has not changed except that it is now cleaner than it was in the smoky air of the first half of the 20th century. The cathedral dome and the Burnaby obelisk now compete for attention on the skyline with John Madin's 20-storey NatWest tower in Colmore Row. National Lottery funding at the turn of the millennium has enabled the diocese to renew the footpaths in stone and tidy up the gravestones in the churchyard. The lawns are so popular with office workers at lunch-time and with young people gathering to meet at other times that in places the grass has almost been worn away. Nevertheless the church and its semi-private surroundings together comprise one of the best civic spaces in the city centre. There are regular lunch-time recitals and other events in the cathedral for city workers and visitors.

BIRMINGHAM SCHOOL OF ART

This magnificent building is considered to be J. H. Chamberlain's masterpiece

Left: The view taken around 1900 from the junction of Margaret Street and Edmund Street shows the full extent of the magnificent College of Arts and Crafts designed by Birmingham architects Martin and Chamberlain in 1881–85. The decorative sculpture and the big rose window on the far left-hand gable are especially fine examples of Arts and Crafts and Art Nouveau styles. The building was extended in 1893 down Cornwall Street, which is on the side furthest away from the camera. The Art School was also where architects were trained between 1909 and 1971, when the Birmingham School of Architecture was established in the new Perry Barr campus of the City of Birmingham Polytechnic.

Above: The Council House extension built in 1917 now occupies the vacant site shown on the left of the c. 1900 photo. At present the School of Art building is still occupied by the Birmingham Institute of Art and Design, a part of Birmingham City University since 2007, but there are proposals to move it to a new campus in Eastside adjacent to Millennium Point. The future use of the School of Art building is uncertain but its Grade 1 listing should ensure that its architectural splendour is maintained for future generations to enjoy. Inside there is a museum which was restored in 1996 and which shows the rich Gothic decoration and construction of the building at their very best.

GREAT WESTERN ARCADE
A well-preserved example of the Victorian shopping arcade

Left: Arcades are the ancestors of the indoor shopping centres or covered 'malls' that can be seen in and on the edges of most of our old city centres. The Great Western Arcade photographed here in 1939 was built in 1875–76 on iron arches over a cutting made for the new railway line from Oxford and Paddington to Snow Hill Station and the Black Country. The line between Temple Row and Moor Street Station was laid in a tunnel but the North Western Arcade was built over it in 1884 to connect Temple Row with Corporation Street. The first shop on the right, Freeman Hardy and Willis, had been selling shoes here since 1876.

Above: The cast iron roof and the upper part of the Great Western Arcade were destroyed by enemy bombs during the war in 1940. The roof was rebuilt in the modern style by the John Madin Design Group in 1985. The floor has been laid with panels of red and white tiles set in dark grey borders and the arcade has managed to keep its Victorian character. The modestly sized shop units are nearly always fully let and the arcade provides a pleasant rain-free passageway between Temple Row and Colmore Row. The North Western Arcade was demolished for the new Rackhams department store in the 1960s and replaced by a modern arcade which incorporates a side entrance to Rackhams (now House of Fraser).

VICTORIA LAW COURTS

This architectural tour-de-force reminds us of the power of the law

Left: The City of Birmingham acquired this symbol of civic pride in 1891 when the Prince and Princess of Wales opened the building whose foundation stone had been laid by the Queen Victoria herself in 1887. Before that, Birmingham's major civil and criminal cases had to be heard at Warwick. The Council Committee wanted Alfred Waterhouse to design the building because of the success of his Assize Courts in Manchester, but the local architects demanded that a competition be held and Waterhouse became one of the judges instead. The winners were Aston Webb and Ingress Bell from London. The whole building is faced in red terracotta made from clay at Ruabon in North Wales. The choice of material allowed the architects to create richly detailed ornament because it was cast in moulds, not carved from natural stone. The inset image shows an internal corridor with a richly ornate balcony.

Above: Since the opening of the Queen Elizabeth II Law Courts in James Watt Street in 1987, the role of the grand old Victoria Law Courts has been reduced to that of a Magistrates' Court. The new court buildings, designed by the government architects, speak of a very different era in which there is no attempt to impress the world at large with the status of the city. A proposal to build a new 'modern' block of magistrates' courts at Eastside was made public in 2008 but the scheme was cut from government spending plans because of the economic crisis. In the meantime the old building, with some modern adaptations such as airport-type security check-points, maintains a dignified presence in one end of Corporation Street opposite its red terracotta cousin, the now forlorn Methodist Central Hall.

CORPORATION STREET

This impressive sweep of Victorian buildings has remained mostly intact

Left: The grandeur of the gently curving Corporation Street is the closest Birmingham got to the Parisian boulevards that cut through inner-city slums in the 19th century. This impressive thoroughfare was a potent symbol of the power that Mayor Joseph Chamberlain deployed over his fellow councillors when the Corporation really ran the city and all of its public services. This viewpoint is from an upper floor of one of the buildings on the east side of the street, near to New Street. Two side streets are just visible on the left (west) side of the street. The entrance to Fore Street runs between the towers of Lloyds Bank and Pattison's Café (with its white awning). Cherry Street appears further along, next to the Cobden Hotel. There are no trams, but a Midland Red bus and a Corporation bus head north along with all the other one-way traffic. The canopy to the left of the first bus belongs to a Yates's Wine Lodge.

Above: The name and alignment of Corporation Street has survived the post-war demolition mania and most of its old buildings remain intact. The three blocks separated by Fore Street and Cherry Street in the old picture are largely unchanged except for the shop fronts. Now mostly obscured by trees, you can still just make out the red tower of the old Lloyds building – Pattison's tower has been removed. The 20-storey, grey-sided Bank House in Cherry Street now overtops the facades on the left. There are some gaps where developers have been able to acquire land for new schemes, but large parts are still owned by the City Council, especially at the northern end of Corporation Street around the Magistrates' Court. In 2012 the Council closed Corporation Street to traffic to begin work on laying the Metro tramlines from Snow Hill to New Street Station.

OLD SQUARE

Originally the site of the medieval Priory of St Thomas of Canterbury

Above: Old Square was originally the site of the Priory (or Hospital) of St Thomas of Canterbury. The priory, which was founded in the 13th century, was dissolved under Henry VIII's Suppression of the Monasteries in 1536–41. The site of the priory was left in ruins until John Pemberton started to built his Priory Estate there 1697. Old Square became the centre of his estate and was the first planned development in the city. Corporation Street reached it from New Street in 1885. In this photo, taken around 1900, the big building with the curved facade and the clock is Newbury's, the draper's warehouse. It was clearly designed to draw maximum attention to itself with its twin turrets and big dome. The small street on the left in sunlight is The Minories and the one ahead is Upper Priory. The buildings in sunlight at the end of the street are in Steelhouse Lane.

Right: Nothing remains of Old Square's 19th-century buildings today. Lewis's department store acquired and demolished the grand Newbury building in the 1920s. Lewis's developed its store over both sides of The Minories, with high-level bridges connecting each side of the building. Lewis's, which had become a big part of Birmingham's retail history, went out of business in 1991 and sold the buildings to property developers. The buildings were refurbished into the high-class offices shown here. Since 1996 Old Square has been the location of a two-dimensional sculpture of Birmingham comedy actor Tony Hancock by Bruce Williams (inset). On the north side of the square there is a wall mural depicting Quakers who were associated with this area, including Charles Lloyd (1748–1819) whose father Sampson Lloyd II founded Lloyds Bank with John Taylor in Birmingham in 1765.

STEELHOUSE LANE /
COLMORE SQUARE
This street has changed beyond recognition

Left: In the 18th century, a 'steelhouse' was set up
by Kettle, Samuel Garbett was refining metals in a
workshop and Farmer & Galton were operating as
merchants and gunmakers at this location. The 1965
view on the left shows the Gaumont Palace cinema,
which stood on the north side of Steelhouse Lane on
the corner of Weaman Street. It was opened in 1931
and designed in the fashionable Art Deco style by W. T.
Benslyn who later designed the first truly Modernist
building in Birmingham, the Brearley Street School.
Behind the cinema rises the tower block of the 1966
Birmingham Post and Mail with the two-storey podium
emerging on the right. The 1905 photo of Steelhouse
Lane above was taken from the junction of Snow Hill
and Bull Street looking east out of town. The most
significant building on the left is the headquarters of
Wesleyan and General Assurance, started by Methodists
in Birmingham in 1841 and incorporated in 1866.

Right: Steelhouse Lane has changed more than
most streets in Birmingham. A Civic Society blue
plaque reminds passers-by that Matthew Boulton
(1728–1809), pioneer of the Industrial Revolution and
founder of the Boulton & Watt steam engine company
with James Watt, was born near here. The post-
modern headquarters of the Wesleyan and General
occupy the site of its own earlier building on the left
of the new Colmore Square. Everything else has gone.
In Steelhouse Lane the Police Station was built on
the site of Ebenezer Chapel and modern barristers'
chambers now cluster round the Victoria Law Courts.
The Gaumont was closed in 1983 and demolished soon
after. The Post and Mail building was demolished in
2005 and replaced by Colmore Plaza in 2007.

GENERAL HOSPITAL
Now the Diana, Princess of Wales Children's Hospital

Left: The first General Hospital was opened in 1779 in Summer Lane and was funded by the proceeds of the Birmingham Triennial Music Festival. It closed in 1897 and was replaced by this new and bigger General Hospital in Steelhouse Lane. It is seen here being opened in grand style in 1897 by Prince Christian Schleswig-Holstein (1831–1917) who became a member of the British Royal family by marrying the Queen's daughter, Princess Helena. A large retinue is seen in the photograph arriving at the original carriage entrance. The E-shaped building designed by William Henman has been described by the architectural historian Kenneth Powell as 'an exuberant Victorian complex in rich red brick and terracotta'.

Above: Following its closure in 1993, the General Hospital was refurbished and reopened in 1998 as the Diana, Princess of Wales Children's Hospital. The modern photograph shows that there have been many alterations to the original building whilst it was the General Hospital although the ornate octagonal ventilation tower has survived. The most recent addition is the 1997 glass entrance canopy, the last project completed by London architects Powell and Moya. There is a landing pad for helicopters nearby on Steelhouse Lane. When the helicopter arrives the street has to be closed to traffic by police who are conveniently stationed opposite the main gate of the hospital.

ST CHAD'S CATHEDRAL

The first Roman Catholic cathedral to be built in England after the Reformation

Left: St Chad's Cathedral was built between 1839 and 1841 on the site of an earlier church just beyond the city centre. Its architect, the renowned Edward Welby Pugin, set out to revive the medieval Gothic style. The cathedral and adjoining Bishop's House were built by Pugin's master builder George Myers. The cathedral included floor tiles by Herbert Minton and silverware by John Hardman Junior. The main photograph from the 1960s shows the cathedral isolated in a sea of cabins and piles of materials belonging to the contractors building the Queensway. A brave attempt was made by the Council in the 1960s to brighten up pedestrian underpasses by commissioning artists to do colourful murals on their walls. The inset image above shows Kenneth Budd's 1968 mosaic mural commemorating the life of the assassinated US President J. F. Kennedy. The mural was paid for by Birmingham's large Irish community. The 12m (40ft) x 3m (9ft) mural depicting diverse races and cultures living together in peace was installed on the convex curving wall of an underpass within sight of the cathedral.

Above: The construction of St Chad's Queensway in the late 1960s demanded the demolition of the Bishop's House. The new St Chad's Queensway cut the cathedral off from the city centre, making it more isolated visually and physically than it was before. Luckily the cathedral itself has remained intact and in a beautiful condition inside and out. Its immediate surroundings have recently been landscaped in connection with the remodelling of St Chad's Circus. An unhappy consequence of the policy of filling in pedestrian underpasses was the loss of some fine works of art that adorned their walls. The Kennedy mural was ripped out by contractors in 2007. Fortunately parts of it were rescued by Oliver Budd, the son of the artist, who has been painstakingly rebuilding it from the original drawings in his studio in East Sussex. A proposal to re-install it in a new square in Digbeth's Irish Quarter, which would be a fitting location in recognition of Kennedy's Irish ancestry, is still awaiting approval.

ALBERT STREET
Only two small sections of Albert Street remain

Left: Albert Street was, as the name suggests, Victorian in origin and was cut through the older streets to connect the northern end of Park Street and High Street where it joined Dale End. This early 1950s photograph is looking west uphill to High Street. The presence of a tram indicates that the picture was taken before 1953. The Salvation Army Hostel for men is the rounded corner building at 113 Moor Street, opposite W. Little & Sons, Boot Manufacturers & Leather Merchants, at number 52. The tall Queen Anne style building with four dormer windows (28–34 Albert Street) dates to 1888. It was built by Arthur Harrison for William Marston, a carriage upholstery manufacturer.

Above: Only two sections of Albert Street remain, one to the east of the Queensway leading to Curzon Street and Millennium Point, and one to the west leading up to Dale End to arrive just to the north of where the original Albert Street arrived. William Marston's building is still there. His carriage and car upholstery company continued to operate from 28–34 Albert Street until 1987. The company, renamed William Marston Limited & Culverhouse & Sons Limited, is now based in Fazeley Street and currently manufactures upholstery for cars, boats and caravans. The Salvation Army hostel moved to the other side of the city in the appropriately named William Booth Lane. The area to the east of Moor Street Queensway has been renamed Eastside. The Council was keen to regenerate this former industrial zone by demolishing the elevated section of Moor Street Queensway, which has since been re-modelled as a tree-lined boulevard where pedestrians and slow-moving vehicles share the same ground.

HIGH STREET

The Martineau Galleries had replaced much of this view by the mid 1960s

Left: This 1960 view is of High Street with Carrs Lane near right. Ahead, Dale End branches to the right of Preedy's the tobacconist and Bull Street branches to its left. The modern four-storey building on the left is the 1959–65 development designed by Seymour Harris & Partners, about to open as Littlewoods. In the main part of High Street behind the camera, Marks and Spencer and the Co-op occupy key positions with their big city-centre department stores.

Above: The shop fronts on the left were redesigned in 1999–2001 but the upper facade seen in the old photo has been retained. All the other buildings were demolished soon after the photo was taken. Work began on building the Martineau Galleries complex, which was designed by Frederick Gibberd in 1963 and completed in 1966. The part of High Street behind this viewpoint was completely pedestrianised, while Bull Street, Dale End and Carrs Lane remained open to buses until 2012 when work began on laying the Metro tramlines along Corporation Street to connect New Street Station and Snow Hill Station. The Co-op department store closed down in the 1980s and the new Pavilions shopping mall opened in its place in 1988.

BULLRING CENTRE
Once the epitome of the ultra-modern shopping centre

Left: When it was opened by the Duke of Edinburgh in 1967 the Bullring shopping centre was thought to be the very latest thing and the people of Birmingham were intensely proud of its ultra modern appearance. The main photograph was taken in the 1970s from the open market looking towards the Rotunda, which floats high over the flat roof of the shopping centre. Times furniture store and Burton advertise their presence on the High Street on the far right of the picture. The white slab above the street stalls is the Ring Road, which cut through the shopping centre. The symbol of the bull clearly identifies the Bullring Centre in the inset photo taken soon after its completion and shown from the other side of the Digbeth dual carriageway. The set of doors below and to the left of the bull open into the main shopping centre and a spiral footbridge leads shoppers to an upper level and the multi-storey car park identified by the windowless facade that looks like a loud speaker.

Right: The 1960s Bullring Centre was demolished in 1999 and the new Bullring opened in its place in 2003. It incorporates an anchor store at each end of its three-tier mall – Selfridges to the east and Debenhams to the west. The Rotunda was rescued from demolition by popular demand, but instead of housing office workers it now houses city-dwellers who can gaze from luxury apartments through floor-to-ceiling windows over the city below. Such is the scale of change here that it is impossible to imagine exactly where the old buildings once stood as you are walking around the shiny new malls and pedestrian areas. Even in the few years since the new Bullring Centre was opened the open space has been redeveloped as Spiceal Street.

ST MARTIN'S CHURCH
Now hemmed in by the new Bullring Centre

Left: Although there has been a church on the site since medieval times, what can be seen in this photograph is quite a recent chapter in the story of its life. The tower and spire had been completely restored and re-faced a mere 100 years before this photograph was taken, after which the rest of the church was carefully demolished and entirely rebuilt 25 years later under the care of architect J. A. Chatwin. The famous Pre-Raphaelite artist Edward Burne-Jones designed the stained-glass south transept window which was made by Morris & Co and installed in 1877. This photograph taken in 1959 shows St Martin's Church before it was hemmed in by the imminent redevelopment of the Bullring. Jamaica Row heads downhill to the right of the church and Digbeth heads off on the left. Lord Nelson's monument, surrounded by scaffolding, stands in front of the church with Midland Red buses circling behind it.

Above: The stonework of St Martin's Church was scrubbed clean and a new storey added to the south west extension during the building of the second Bullring Centre in 2003. The exterior of the church is otherwise unchanged, unlike the surrounding streets and buildings. The entrance under the west tower is now completely pedestrianised, and the view of the north side of the church can only be seen beyond the new balcony from between the two malls of the new Bullring. In 2001 archaeologists from Birmingham University exhumed the human remains from 857 burials in the graveyard on the north side of the church to prepare the ground for the new Bullring. Those whose names were known were re-buried on the site and those that were unidentified were re-buried at Quinton cemetery. Lord Nelson's statue has been restored to a place not far from where it was in the earlier picture.

BULLRING STREET MARKET
A street market has been held in and around this area since the 12th century

Left: There seems to be only a poor remnant of a thriving street market here in this black and white photograph from 1939. However, it was usual for old street markets to take place literally on the street without any permanent or portable stalls. This view is taken from the steps in front of the Market Hall, looking south past the statue of Lord Nelson towards Digbeth. A tram is entering Moor Street on the left and the edge of St Martin's Church is just visible on the far right beyond Nelson. The faint cupola in the distance is the Police Station on the corner of Allison Street. A street market has been held in and around this area since the 12th century but in the 20th century it has had to struggle against the pressures of redevelopment and competition from chain stores, supermarkets, department stores and indoor shopping centres. The colour inset image was taken in 1959 on the last day of the Bullring street market, before the redevelopment of the Bullring began in earnest. The view is uphill towards the junction of High Street and New Street where a multi-storey office block and a three storey shop show that the redevelopment of the city centre had already begun. The Market Hall, with its grand Doric-columns, is at the top left-hand side of the street.

Above: The original 1950s viewpoint is now buried below the East Mall Bullring Shopping Centre. Everything in the picture except St Martin's Church and the Police Station was swept away in the 1960s. The statue of Nelson was moved to a balcony in the new development and moved again in 2000 to another balcony overlooking St Martin's Church, only 20 or 30 metres to the south west of the old viewpoint and about the same distance west of its original location. The closest viewpoint from which to recreate the early 1950s photo is the balcony outside Selfridges where it is still possible to see the cupola of the Police Station. The inset image shows that the modern office block and the shop building at the junction of High Street and New Street are the same but everything else, including the magnificent Market Hall, has changed.

MARKET HALL

Charles Edge's Market Hall was demolished to make way for the new Bullring Centre

Left: Before the turn of the 19th century, small traders sold corn and vegetables in the open air on the streets and pavements of the Bullring. However, the need for an organised publicly owned market hall was considered necessary to cope with the rapid growth in the city's population in the first half of that century. The result was the splendid Market Hall designed in the massive Doric style, the front of which is seen here in 1901, and built by the Street Commissioners to the designs of Charles Edge, 1832–35. The vast hall accommodated 600 stalls for traders who would otherwise have crowded the streets and pavements in unregulated confusion. The inset photograph shows the rear facade of the Market Hall in Worcester Street, which faced New Street Station. It was almost as grand as the front but it was not the traditional place for street traders. The photo suggests it was more of a meeting place for cabbies as it was opposite the carriageway into the station known as Queen's Drive.

Above: During a Second World War air raid, the roof was destroyed but it was not until 1958 that the council began to plan its replacement by a modernistic Bullring Shopping Centre. The pedestrian street between the East and West Malls of the present-day Bullring Centre follows fairly closely the line of the old High Street from where the 1901 photo was taken. There is no market hall here today but there is a new Indoor Market in the block defined by Gloucester Street, Edgbaston Street, Pershore Street and Upper Dean Street. Although it is not on the same scale as the original, it is nevertheless meeting a lively demand for low-cost goods and sustaining the many small individual traders that survive despite the presence of supermarkets and department stores all around. It was designed by the council's own architects and opened in 2000. Many other street traders continue to operate in the Outdoor Market although like their colleagues in the Wholesale Market, they are anxious about their future in a spot that has seen an open-air market since 1166.

FISH MARKET

Widespread methods of refrigeration reduced the need for a fresh fish market

Left: The Fish Market was built in 1869–71 to the designs of local architect John Jones Bateman (1817–1903). The market faced the High Street and was separated from Market Hall by Bell Street. This photo was taken near to where Nelson's statue stood until the 1960s (see page 57) and looks south down the hill towards Smithfield Market and Digbeth. The slow-moving horse and cart mixes easily with people on foot. Small traders would sell local produce from their baskets on the pavement in the open air, but fish was brought by rail over a hundred miles from Grimsby or Fleetwood to be sold in the covered Fish Market. Although ice was used, mechanical refrigeration was still in its infancy. The traditional character of the marketplace was maintained by its diversity and small scale of its occupants – the names Prince of Wales, a public house, and Mortons can be picked out in this c. 1885 photo.

Above: Cleared for the first Bullring Centre, the site of the old Fish Market now lies underneath the second Bullring Shopping Mall. With the advent of refrigerated lorries, supermarket, shop and domestic refrigerators and freezers, fish can now be frozen solid, preserved indefinitely and transported long distances. Consequently, the need for a big market selling fresh fish gradually disappeared. Since 2003 the retail fish market has been incorporated in the Bullring Indoor Market in Gloucester Street. This modern building has 80 stalls selling all kinds of produce undercover.

SMALLBROOK QUEENSWAY
Birmingham's Inner Ring Road was later dubbed 'the concrete collar'

Left: The Inner Ring Road was renamed Queensway after it was fully completed and opened by the Queen in 1971. This gently curved section, Smallbrook Queensway, is seen here in 1972. It is lined on the left side with the longest office block in Birmingham, designed by the Rotunda architect James Roberts in 1958–62. His solution, which was favoured by the city's planners at the time, contrasts with that adopted on the Hagley Road, where free-standing tower blocks are set back from the road on their own landscaped plot. The change in the design of the facade on the left marks the point where the building crosses Hurst Street. The Ring Road was actually elevated over the valley of the Smallbrook to allow pedestrians to cross underneath it safely but without much pleasure. The twin blocks at the end of the street are the City Council's 32-storey residential Sentinel Towers (1968–71) also by James Roberts. The scene is entirely modern and although it contains a wide variety of shapes and sizes of buildings, it does have a certain calmness due to the use of a common architectural language.

Above: In 2003 work began on the 40-storey, post-modern green glass Beetham Tower, incorporating the Radisson Hotel and various apartments. The tower, which looms over Holloway Circus, can be seen on the right. Post-modern architects often reject the constraints that modernist architects imposed on themselves to produce a harmonious ensemble of buildings. The idea of keeping pedestrians and fast-moving vehicles strictly apart went out of favour after a conference of urban design experts meeting at Highbury recommended that the Ring Road should be downgraded. Although Queensway was at first hailed as a revolutionary approach to urban design, council planners eventually began to view it as a 'concrete collar' and an obstacle to further development. In Smallbrook Queensway this led to the lowering of the elevated section, which allowed pedestrians to take their chances crossing the road once again.

BIRMINGHAM, CIVIC CENTRE & HALL OF MEMORY

V 7691

BASKERVILLE HOUSE
Originally intended as the first phase of Birmingham's Civic Centre

Above: Baskerville House, on the left, was named after John Baskerville (1706–75), the Birmingham printer who invented the typeface that bears his name. Completed in 1940, Baskerville House was intended to be just the first phase, the east wing, of an ambitious plan for a new L-shaped Civic Centre. With the intervention of the Second World War and the period of austerity that followed in the 1950s the Council's grand scheme was abandoned. The open space in front of Baskerville House was to have been part of a huge square marked by a column 42m (140 ft) high with a nude male statue on top representing the Spirit of Birmingham. On the right is the Hall of Memory, the first building in the scheme to be completed in 1925. In the gap between the two civic buildings can be seen a terrace of older properties around Suffolk Street and Great Charles Street.

Right: Baskerville House was occupied by the City's Economic Development and Planning Departments until the 1990s when they were moved to Alpha Tower. After standing empty for several years, the Grade II listed building was sold to a property developer who converted it into commercial offices and added a glazed penthouse on the top. The Council briefly considered using part or all of this building for the Central Library to move into, but in 2006 it decided to build a new library on the site next to Baskerville House, which had been a ground-level car park for many years. A large-scale version of Baskerville's typeface stands in front of the building. The gap on the left of the Hall of Memory is now filled by the black glass facade of the Copthorne Hotel, with the BT Tower rising above it. Albert Toft's statue of Edward VII – recently brought back from Highgate Park, where it had been since it was removed from Victoria Square in 1951 – now stands outside the right-hand corner of Baskerville House. The building on the right of the Hall of Memory is the Central Library, opened in 1974 and reached by a footbridge over Paradise Circus Queensway.

BINGLEY HALL / INTERNATIONAL CONVENTION CENTRE

Britain's first purpose-built exhibition hall

Left: Bingley Hall, Britain's first purpose-built exhibition hall, was designed by Birmingham architect J. A. Chatwin. It was opened in 1850, a year before Prince Albert's Great Exhibition of 1851 in the Crystal Palace erected in London's Hyde Park. These hugely popular exhibitions showcased the many and varied products that British manufacturers were offering to the public and the world at large. Before 1850, exhibitions in Birmingham were held in a wooden hut in the grounds of Bingley House (1760). Bingley Hall was built on the site of the former house. This photo of Bingley Hall's Central Avenue was taken during an exhibition in 1886.

Right: Bingley Hall was destroyed by fire in 1984. It was considered not worthwhile to rebuild it as its function had already been taken over by the City Council's new National Exhibition Centre (NEC). The site of Bingley Hall is now occupied not by the NEC, which was built instead on farmland east of the city and opened by the Queen in 1976, but by the International Convention Centre (ICC) that was also opened by the Queen, but much later in 1991. It is interesting to speculate as to whether the designers of the ICC were inspired to emulate the old Central Avenue with their elongated glazed atrium that offers a covered way between Centenary Square and the canal. The canal is crossed by a footbridge to reach the Waters Edge in Brindleplace, a spot made famous when Bill Clinton was photographed by the world's press drinking a beer there during a break in the 1998 G8 Summit. The colonnade that once stood in Centenary Square was re-located to make way for the brick paving designed by Tess Jaray and the *Forward* sculpture by Richard Mason, since destroyed by fire.

GAS STREET BASIN
This busy trading canal was overtaken by rail and then road transport by the 1960s

Left: When this photo was taken in the 1950s Gas Street Basin was bleak and forlorn. Gas Street was named after John Gosling's gasworks that stood close by. The heyday of canal transport, the late 18th century, when a hundred barges a day passed through the city, is long gone. The narrowboat *George* passes through the Worcester Bar lock on its way under Broad Street to Old Turn Junction. At the junction, it joined the canal that encircled the city centre and from which the main canals carried barges to all points of the compass. Building over a canal was quite unusual and was brought about by the rapid development of both sides of Broad Street. The gabled building over the canal was designed by Martin and Chamberlain toward the end of the 19th century. The tower behind, which is only just visible through the mist, is the Chapel of the Messiah. The top two floors and the chimney stack of William Butler's brewery also appear faintly to the right of the chapel and behind the white roofs of the buildings on Broad Street.

Above: The lock gate is gone along with the historic rivalry between the canal companies. The chapel and the brewery have been demolished but the Martin and Chamberlain building is still visible in the distance. The restoration of the surrounding buildings was completed in the 1990s. The top of the International Convention Centre and the Symphony Hall appear beyond the old chimney stack. Brindleyplace, the Sea Life Centre and the National Indoor Arena are a short walk through the Broad Street tunnel. The dark glass skyscraper on the right edge of the photograph is the Hyatt Hotel. These developments have transformed the city centre canals and the Gas Street Basin into a popular tourist spot for walkers, bikers and canal users. Far left is the Canalside Café, a pub and café housed in a lock-keeper's cottage that dates to 1770. Gas Street still carries its original name although coal gas is no longer produced here. The restored Retort House, a former gasworks, is out of sight a few yards away down Gas Street awaiting a new use and a new occupier.

CRESCENT THEATRE / BRINDLEYPLACE

The Crescent Theatre is now at the heart of Brindleyplace

Left: This 1968 photo shows the Crescent Theatre, which opened in Cumberland Street in 1964. The story of the theatre company is one of remarkable determination by a band of Council employees who formed the Municipal Players in 1923 to put on plays in whatever venue they could find, including the Council House canteen. The theatre company's name derives from their first premises, in three empty houses on The Crescent. The Crescent was a speculative development started in 1795 to create an elegant row of Georgian town houses. The architectural historian Pevsner wrote in 1966 that The Crescent failed because there was no rich and leisured class within the city. When the Municipal Players left The Crescent, the Council offered them a new site on Cumberland Street. Their new theatre was designed by Graham Winteringham, the architect of the Birmingham REP. The buildings rising above the theatre are the Victorian ventilation tower of the Oozells Street School and the modern office block on Broad Street designed by John Madin in 1966 and known as Rail House.

Above: The theatre's first home, The Crescent, was demolished and replaced by Brindley Walk and a row of council tower blocks north of Cambridge Street, one of which was named Crescent Tower. In the late 1980s, the Council sold the theatre's Cumberland Street site to a developer who agreed to provide a new theatre in its plans for Brindleyplace. The replacement theatre, which opened in 1998, is shown here in what became Sheepcote Street. The theatre's old Cumberland Street site was redeveloped and incorporated into Brindleyplace. Both Oozells Street School and Rail House (now Quayside Tower) still exist but are out of sight in this photo. The school is now the Ikon Gallery (see inset), which was retained in the new development and now stands in the heart of Brindleyplace. A new office block designed by Glenn Howells is seen rising above the Hilton Garden Hotel. By 1998 the Birmingham Civic Society was so impressed with the design of Brindleyplace that it awarded its owners, Argent Group, its annual Forward Prize for its work.

VYSE STREET, THE JEWELLERY QUARTER

The Chamberlain Clock is the Jewellery Quarter's main landmark

Left: Gold and silver have been worked in this district for over two hundred years, but the trade really began as the 'toy', small goods, trade that made buckles, buttons and trinkets. Brummagem Toys were produced in hundreds of thousands in cut steel, brass and silver. This view along Vyse Street was taken in 1967 with the cast iron Chamberlain Memorial Clock in the distance. The 1950s inset image shows the clock at the junction of Warstone Lane and Vyse Street. It has stood at the heart of Birmingham's jewellery district since 1903 when it was erected to commemorate Joseph Chamberlain's visit to South Africa. Demand for jewellery peaked in 1920 after which a slow decline began. By the time this photograph was taken the business association was already planning to redevelop the district with modern factory buildings. Just out of frame is the Church of England Warstone Lane Cemetery opened in 1848 and where, in amongst the catacombs, are remains of John Baskerville, printer and typeface inventor, and Major Harry Gent, the inventor of lawn tennis.

Above: The Jewellery Quarter is now a Conservation Area and has its own development agency that promotes the businesses and argues for policies that respect its architectural heritage. A Museum of the Jewellery Quarter has been created in what was the jewellery factory of Smith & Pepper at 78–80 Vyse Street and an octagonal visitor information centre, designed by students of the Prince of Wales Institute, was opened in 1997 outside the flatted factory known as the Big Peg. The Big Peg (the tall building on the left) and the multi-storey carpark replaced the terrace of workshops in the early 1970s. The Chamberlain Clock is in the same place at the end of the street. The clock tower was preserved, but other parts of Vyse Street were demolished. The public house on the corner of Vyse Street and Warstone Lane (see inset) is the 1920s Rose Villa Tavern, with its original Poole Pottery tiled interior.

ST PAUL'S SQUARE

The motor industry has made way for the music industry in these Georgian buildings

Left: This three-storey terrace is part of the south-east side of St Paul's Square, the rest of which, including St Paul's Church, is out of sight to the right of this photograph. The street at the end is Ludgate Hill, which runs south east to the city centre. Although St Paul's Square was built as a residential square in 1790 on land once owned by the Colmore family, it was soon occupied by small-scale manufacturing businesses. St Paul's Church was built in 1771 to the design of Roger Eykin and was where steam-engine manufacturers Matthew Boulton and James Watt owned box pews and regularly worshipped. A painted window of the Conversion of St Paul was made by Francis Eginton who worked for Boulton at his Staffordshire metal goods manufactory for many years. The section of St Paul's Square seen in the photo – numbers 3, 5, 7 and 9, comprising the Victory Works of W. J. Hill – was clearly not residential when this 1953 photo was taken. The firm specialised in lighting and accessories for motor vehicles and bicycles.

Above: The Georgian facades have survived intact but the nameplates indicate that they are no longer occupied by metalworking businesses. St Paul's Square is now the only remaining Georgian square in the city. Numbers 3 and 5 comprise the Jam House, a live music venue with capacity for six hundred jazz, blues or rock enthusiasts. The Jam House, which opened in 1999, was formed by pianist Jools Holland and designer Neil Tibbatt who wanted to create a live music venue that combined 'unplugged' live performances and fine dining. There is now space for 220 to dine formally or 150 to dine 'theatre-style'. The interior and the back yards have been extensively remodelled for the venue's new role, but the result is a testimony to the durability, adaptability and continuing popularity of these old buildings.

LUDGATE HILL

This once-industrial street is now filled with bars and restaurants

Left: Ludgate Hill runs downhill from St Paul's Square, crossing Water Street, then the Birmingham and Fazeley Canal and Lionel Street before climbing to Great Charles Street. There it becomes Church Street leading to Colmore Row and St Philip's Cathedral, which is hidden from view by the bend in the street. Ludgate Hill, photographed here in 1960, is one of the principal streets of the Newhall estate, which was owned by St Thomas's Priory in the Middle Ages and acquired by the Colmore family in the 16th century. It tends to be the poor relation of Newhall Street, home of the important Assay Office and the former Elkington electro-plating factory. Ludgate Hill is lined by modest 19th- and 20th-century industrial premises, including an 1854 warehouse at number 21, a 1912 factory at number 17 built by De Lacy Aherne, and the 1898 bank building (visible far right in the photo above) that boasts a Jacobean entrance and a noteworthy oriel window.

Above: The row of bollards, the gas street lamp and the near view of the street beyond look much the same, but the skyline is now punctuated by a number of sleek city centre office blocks partially hidden by a mature tree. Most buildings have found a new use. A stroll down Ludgate Hill will reveal that nearly every building as far as Lionel Street has become a stylish bar or gourmet restaurant complete with continental-style pavement cafés. The building at number 21 is now a bar and bistro while number 17 was converted and extended in 1997 by architect Mark Humphries to create Ludgate Lofts – a mixture of modern flats and loft apartments.

MOOR STREET STATION

Trains now run to London from this former terminus for local services

Left: Moor Street Station was opened by the Great Western Railway in 1909 to relieve pressure on the two-track tunnel into Snow Hill Station. It was not until 1914 that permanent station buildings were erected. Immediate clues to the 1986 date of this picture are the Pavilions shopping centre, seen here under construction prior to its opening in 1988, and the diesel railcar on the platform far left. There are no signs of the portal to the Snow Hill tunnel to the right of the multi-gabled station buildings as the line to Snow Hill had been closed since 1968 as part of the Beeching cuts. Moor Street Station at the time of this photo was used only as a terminus for local services to Stratford-upon-Avon and Leamington Spa.

Above: Grants from the European Regional Development Fund were used to pay for the tunnel to Snow Hill to be re-opened in 1995. Moor Street Station was renovated in 2002 in its original style by the Birmingham Alliance and Chiltern Railways at a cost of £11 million. Platform 4 was re-opened in 2010. The station is used by London Midland and Chiltern Railways to run services between Birmingham and London. London Midland also run trains to Smethwick, Stourbridge Worcester and Hereford via Snow Hill. Passengers arriving at Moor Street are now advised to alight here for the Bullring shopping centre. The curvaceous aluminium building on the left belongs to Selfridges. Often seen as a symbol of Birmingham's regeneration, this Bullring Centre department store was completed in 2003 at a cost of £60 million.

DIGBETH

Now a part of the city centre, Digbeth offers views of Birmingham's key landmarks

Left: The horse-drawn milk float, the Midland Red single-deck bus, the helmeted policeman on point duty, the granite setts on the road and the redundant-looking tramlines of this 1954 photo will evoke strong memories for some. St Martin's Church is the obvious landmark in the distance, almost obscured by rain, fog or pollution. On the right, on the corner of Allison Street, is the white stone police station with the bowler-hatted clock tower. The building was designed by the City Surveyor in 1911 when the Corporation was in charge of the police. The brick gable end of the Digbeth Cold Store is just visible beyond. The inset view towards the city centre from the dual carriageway of Digbeth in 1968 includes the curved brick building of Digbeth Coach Station on the left, the spire of St Martin's Church and the recently completed Rotunda.

Above: The police station and church of the 1954 image remain durable landmarks amidst a sea of change but the rejuvenated Rotunda now vies with them for attention. The office buildings on the left, the closest of which is named after the long-gone Smithfield Market, occupy the traffic island in the middle. The Cold Store with its gable end fully exposed still stands awaiting refurbishment by the property developers who have now erected blue hoardings around the site of the demolished Midland Red Social Club on the other corner of Allison Street. On the far left in the inset image rises the 40-storey green glass tower of the Radisson Hotel and on the far right sits the shimmering and curvaceous facade of Selfridges in the Bullring Centre.

DIGBETH COACH STATION / BIRMINGHAM COACH STATION

The reconstructed and rebranded coach station was opened by Fabio Capello in 2009

Above: The sign on the bus garage to the right of the handsome curved block in Rea Street, Digbeth, seen here in the 1920s, denotes that it belongs to Midland Red Motor Services. The coach station was established by Midland Red, the popular name for the Birmingham and Midland Motor Omnibus Company, on the site that became known as Digbeth Coach Station. The company was founded in 1905 but by 1912 Birmingham Corporation wanted to run its own buses in Birmingham so an agreement was made with Midland Red that they would concentrate on the rest of the Midlands and only bring passengers to and from Birmingham, thus leaving the Corporation to run buses inside the city boundary. Midland Red started express coach services to Weston-super-Mare and Llandudno in 1921.

Right: The imposing curved building was lost during the boom in coach travel in the late 1950s when the four-storey block on the right of the new white canopy was built. Non-stop coach services to London began when the M1 motorway was opened in 1959. The famous Midland Red name gradually disappeared, first under nationalisation in 1969, then privatisation in 1981. Digbeth Coach Station has been run by National Express since the 1970s. The coach station itself was closed for reconstruction in 2007 and operated from a temporary home in the former Smithfield Garage on the opposite side of the road with an entrance in Oxford Street. The buildings fronting Digbeth were completely refurbished and the site remodelled with public artworks and modern facilities. The re-branded Birmingham Coach Station was officially opened by the then England Football Team Manager Fabio Capello in December 2009. Today National Express serves over 1,000 destinations and carries 18 million passengers a year.

OLD CROWN INN
The oldest secular building in Birmingham

Left: This public house on the corner of Deritend High Street and Heath Mill Lane has been dated to the late 15th century. It was originally built as the Guildhall and School of the Guild of St John the Baptist of Deritend. The brick wall of the ground floor was built in the 19th century, at the same time that the building was converted into an inn. Photographed in 1960, this black and white timber framed building must have been considered very important for it to have survived the changes that transformed Deritend all around it in the 20th century. In the 2005 Pevsner guide to Birmingham, Andy Foster refers to the building's 'civic air, with its close-studded and jettied first floor and central entrance, with a gabled oriel above on big brackets and pilasters'. Its future was secured by becoming a Grade II listed building in 1952.

Above: The Old Crown became the only medieval secular building left in central Birmingham after the 16th-century Golden Lion Inn was moved from Deritend to Cannon Hill Park in 1911. A thorough restoration job was carried out in 1998 leaving the main facade to the High Street largely unaltered. Other alterations behind the timber frame were carried out to modernise its facilities and make the building accessible. The Birmingham Civic Society awarded the Old Crown its Forward Prize for 1999. The Forward Prize is awarded to individuals, organizations, buildings and architectural developments that have made a positive impact on Birmingham. The Crown operates as a hotel with eight rooms available – some en-suite and some with four-poster beds. As it is close to the coach station and the city centre, the Old Crown is very different from the standardised large-scale hotels that are now common in every modern city.

CURZON STREET STATION
A permanent use for this Grade I listed building is yet to be decided

Left: Curzon Street Station was the first mainline railway terminus in Britain. It was designed by Philip Charles Hardwick and built in 1838 in front of the platforms and sheds to mark the Birmingham terminus of the London and Birmingham Railway. By 1841, 11 trains were running between London and Birmingham every day and passengers paid one pound for the five-hour journey. Birmingham's London counterpart, the Euston Arch, although strictly speaking a propylaeum in the Doric order, was also designed by the same architect in 1837 but was demolished in the 1960s when Euston Station was redeveloped. Curzon Street escaped that fate because not long after it was opened the mainline was taken past Curzon Street and through tunnels into the city centre where New Street Station was opened by the London and North Western Railway company in 1852. Curzon Street Station became redundant and isolated but also safe from future redevelopment.

Above: The building on the left has been demolished but the main building is now listed Grade I. It has lain empty for some years after being restored by a group of young trainees under the Community Programme run by the government's Manpower Services Commission. Since then various uses have been proposed but no permanent use has yet emerged. The Royal College of Organists was interested in taking it over, but the latest idea is for it to house a Museum of Photography as part of the Ikon Gallery's plans for a new Museum of Modern Art nearby. The original goods yard behind the station building is being incorporated in the plans for a new high-speed rail terminus. The London to Birmingham HS2 link is scheduled to be completed by 2026.

DIGBETH CANAL

Industry has been replaced by cruising longboats along this stretch of the canal

Left: This photograph was taken in 1968 from the embankment of the main railway line east out of New Street over the roofs of the Birmingham Gun Barrel Proof House. Both the institution and the buildings that house the Proof House date to 1813 when an Act of Parliament authorised a Board of Guardians comprising master gun makers, magistrates and councillors to appoint a Proof Master to supervise the testing of gun barrels and completed guns. The view is south-east towards London, the Grand Union Canal's final destination. Beyond the iron footbridge and the disused railway bridge is a large red-brick building with a curved end, which is a warehouse built by canal carriers Fellows Morton & Clayton that has a road entrance in Fazeley Street. Beyond this is the blue-brick Bond Warehouse that had its own basin and wagon loading yard also opening onto Fazeley Street. Steam is rising around a chimney beside W. Canning's electro-plating works in Great Barr Street.

Above: The railway embankment is now inaccessible to photographers, so this photo is taken from beneath the footbridge seen in the 1968 photo. The huge chimney has disappeared thanks to more stringent environmental regulations. The canalside buildings remain in various degrees of use and the canal itself sees some holiday cruising longboats during the summer. Today Kingfishers can be spotted along this quiet stretch of canal. The Bond Company was formed in 1988 to purchase and renovate the Bond Warehouse so as to provide managed office space and conference facilities. The Fellows Morton & Clayton building now carries the name of Clifton Steel on its Fazeley Street facade. Entry to the Proof House is now through modern security gates at the end of Banbury Street and pedestrian access to the canal towpaths is through an opening in the wall where Fazeley Street crosses over a short spur of the canal.

ASTON HALL

This Grade I listed mansion is the only surviving Jacobean building in Birmingham

Left: Aston Hall is described by Andy Foster in the current Pevsner guide to Birmingham as 'a stranded relic of Birmingham's rural past'. The house looks much the same on the outside as when it was completed in the 1630s. Its first owner was Thomas Holte who began the project in 1618 using plans drawn up by John Thorpe. In 1819 James Watt Junior (1769–1848), the son of the famous engineer James Watt, occupied it for a time. By the end of the 19th century it had passed into the ownership of Birmingham Corporation. Aston Hall is unique on two counts – it is the only surviving building in the Jacobean style in the old County of Warwickshire and it was the first big house of its kind to be taken into public ownership. It had previously been saved from demolition by a committee of working men who set up the Aston Park Company to run the house and grounds as a museum and place of entertainment.

Above: Today Aston Hall is still owned by Birmingham City Council and managed by Birmingham Museum and Art Gallery, although plans are afoot to transfer it to a new charitable trust that will take responsibility for all the city's museums and art galleries. Following a major refurbishment scheme funded by the National Lottery, Aston Hall and grounds are fully open for visitors. While this Grade I listed building has been beautifully restored, part of its easternmost grounds were used in construction of the 1972 Aston Expressway, the A38(M). The house can be hired for candlelight dinners, weddings and children's activities, and every other year it hosts 'Aston Hall by Candlelight', where actors recreate life there in the Jacobean period and the house is lit by 500 candles. Although not visible from this angle, Aston Villa's football stadium is only 200 yards away to the north.

VILLA PARK

Home to Aston Villa Football Club since 1897

Left: When this 1932 photograph was taken most Villa fans were completely exposed to the weather and stood on the terraces for the entire match. This view is taken from a high vantage point at the Witton Road end looking to the Holte End, with the spire of Aston Parish Church on the horizon to the south east. The brick-built stand facing Trinity Road is on the right. The first football clubs were often formed by local church members keen to play sport during the winter when cricket was ruled out. Aston Villa was founded like this in 1874 when men from the Wesleyan Chapel played visiting teams on Aston Lower Grounds. Players were usually recruited from local amateur teams. Aston Villa was a founder member of the Football League in 1888 and Villa Park became its home ground in 1897 at the same time as the terraces of workers' housing sprung up in the surrounding streets. Before the mass-ownership of cars, many supporters would have walked or travelled on buses and trains to get to the match.

Above: Villa Park is now rated a five-star stadium by UEFA, the European governing body of football. Villa became a founder member of the Premier League in 1992 where it has remained since. The 42,788-seat stadium is truly astonishing and the latest developments involved extending over Trinity Road and Witton Lane. Much of the red-brick building on Trinity Road at the Holte End has been retained and reminds us of Aston Villa's long history here. Football is now a huge industry, spectators travel hundreds and even thousands of miles to attend matches and players from all over the world play in the team. The roofs that now extend over the terraces have obscured the earlier views of Aston Parish Church and beyond. While Villa Park has been developed and expanded over the years, much of the old terrace housing surrounding the stadium is still there. A residents' parking scheme now operates in the surrounding streets on match days to cope with the many supporters who arrive by car.

ASTON PARISH CHURCH
The only church in Birmingham to be mentioned in the Domesday Book

Left: This 1968 photograph was taken from the slopes of Aston Park below Aston Hall. The 15th-century spire and tower with its many fine pinnacles and gargoyles, belongs to the Parish Church of St Peter and St Paul, more commonly known as Aston Parish Church. It is the only church in Birmingham that was mentioned in the Domesday Book. The north window of the church has stained glass produced in 1793 by Francis Eginton, who also made a window for St Paul's Church in the Jewellery Quarter. The church shares this scene with the cooling towers and chimneys of Nechells Power Station. Between the church and power station stands a Victorian terrace. A first power station was opened by Birmingham Corporation in Nechells in 1923, when coal was king. A second was opened in 1954, again supplied by rail from the midland coalfields. On the right edge of the photo is Ansell's Brewery, which gave Aston a distinctive aroma on certain days.

Above: The most dramatic change in the scene was the construction of the two-mile-long elevated Aston Expressway or A38(M) in 1972, which linked the city centre with the M6 at Spaghetti Junction. This involved the demolition of many dwellings, including the Victorian terraces and Ansell's Brewery seen in the 1968 photo. The power station has also disappeared, having closed down in 1982. The church and the open space of Aston Park with its fully matured trees provide symbols of endurance and stability. While the Grade II listed church was mostly redesigned by J. A. Chatwin between 1879 and 1890, it contains many old monuments, including an alabaster knight (c. 1360) and a sandstone lady (c. 1490).

95

LUCAS FACTORY / LUCAS CIRCUS

The Lucas factory was integral to the West Midlands' motor manufacturing boom

Left: The Lucas factory, which lined both sides of Great King Street, is decorated for the Coronation of George VI in 1936. The two buildings were connected by a bridge which carries the sign 'In Loyal Tribute'. The founder of the company, Joseph Lucas opened his first workshop to make lamps at 24 Little King Street in 1872. The Lucas factory's 'King of the Road' and 'Silver King' cycle dynamo sets and motor vehicle lamps became world famous. His successors built the business into an essential part of the booming motor manufacturing industry in the West Midlands, making batteries, starter motors and ignition systems.

Above: Lucas employed 28,000 people during the 1950s and 1970s, when it had diversified into military weapons manufacture as Lucas Aerospace. Its workers are remembered for their unsuccessful attempt to save jobs by persuading the company to make socially useful products such as kidney machines rather than military goods. By 1995 the Great King Street factory had been completely demolished and in 1996 the company merged with North American Varity Corporation to form Lucas Varity plc. All that remains on the green at Lucas Circus, between New John Street West and Boulton Middleway, is a commemorative slate obelisk (see inset) with the inscription, 'Lucas Industries Limited. On this site Joseph Lucas established his first workshop – c. 1872 – from small beginnings...'

SPAGHETTI JUNCTION

Now a part of Birmingham's national identity

Left: The multi-level motorway interchange at Gravelly Hill, on the M6 north of the city centre, was completed in 1972. It has remained more or less intact since then and has even become, for better or worse, a part of Birmingham's national identity. The three cooling towers of the aging coal-fired Nechells Power Station stand near the junction where the Aston Expressway, or A38(M), headed into the city centre, which is just out of view beyond the left edge of the photo. The M6 continues on its way past Walsall to the North West out of the top of the photo.

Right: The cooling towers have gone and there is now a rash of new white-roofed sheds beyond the junction. The government's 'dash for gas' in the 1990s sounded the death knell for the power station, although the main turbine hall (out of frame here) remains today. 'Star City', a big American-style entertainment and leisure complex, invented in the late 1990s by the Heartlands Development Corporation to bring new jobs to the Nechells area has taken the place of the cooling towers. In 2008 the city council's director of planning and regeneration was so enamoured with Spaghetti Junction as an icon of the city that he proposed it be floodlit every night to make it visible from space. This has not been done yet, but the underside of the road with its monumental pillars and network of canals and rivers has become an unusual location for artists wanting to mount large-scale installations.

YE OLDE GREEN MAN / THE LAD IN THE LANE

The pub's mock Tudor facade hides a 14th-century timber frame

Left: This group of distinguished and sober-looking ladies and gentlemen pose outside Ye Olde Green Man (also known as The Lad in the Lane) in 1911. They are all members of the Vesey Club, which seems to have been an early Natural History Society attached to Sutton Coldfield Rotarians. Why they are outside a pub in Erdington is a mystery, but perhaps the historic building itself was the purpose of their visit rather than the pub's offer of Rushton's Mild and Pale Ales. The 1996 Pevsner guide to Warwickshire notes that the timber-framed Green Man was 'supposed to have served its present purpose for six centuries'. It is described as having an open hall of two bays divided by a cruck truss, much altered, but probably dating from the 15th century. The sign on this photo claims that the pub was originally established in 1306.

Above: The ancient inn, now known only as The Lad in the Lane, is sandwiched between inter-war, semi-detached houses bordering Bromford Lane. The building was listed Grade II in 1952. There is more of a show of timber on its exterior walls than there was in 1911, but as black and white 'mock Tudor', which became fashionable in stockbroker suburbs around the country. Few passers-by would know whether they were looking at the real thing or a false facade but a scientific method called dendrochronology has been used to date the timbers to the 14th century. Where the Vesey Club members posed is now the car park. The Vesey Club most likely survived into the modern era by merging with the Sutton Coldfield Natural History Society.

JUNCTION INN / BLOOMSBURY ESTATE

This area was cleared and replaced by modern estates in the 1950s

Left: The sign over the ground floor of the Junction Inn indicates that the photograph was taken some years before the Wolverhampton brewer William Butler joined with the Smethwick brewer Henry Mitchell in 1898. The inn stood on the road junction between Bloomsbury Street on the left and Saltley Road on the right. It was also close to the Grand Junction Railway. Opened in 1837 between Birmingham, Crewe and Warrington, the GJR was the country's first trunk railway line and was later taken over by the London and North Western Railway. Tramlines can be seen on Bloomsbury Street as well as two Corporation officials and a tram in the distance. The 1890 Ordnance Survey also shows tramlines along Saltley Road.

Above: The public library, on the far right in the main image, was built in 1892 in Saltley Road. The library was designed by Cossins and Peacock in the red terracotta style that became common around the city. The 20-storey Victor Tower on the left was built in 1969 as part of the Bloomsbury Estate. In the mid 1950s, City Engineer Herbert Manzoni drew up ambitious plans to clear away all the old buildings and construct the modern estates, tower blocks and dual carriageways that we see today. What was Saltley Road in the old photo is now one half of the dual carriageway named Nechells Parkway. In the park nearby, a play sculpture (see inset) reminds people that near here in 1895 the first all-British, four-wheel petrol car was built by Frederick W. Lanchester.

FORT DUNLOP
The world's largest factory when it was completed in 1916

Left: This multi-storey factory known as Fort Dunlop was built in 1916 to cope with the huge demand for solid rubber tyres on military vehicles. Designed by Philip Stott and W. W. Gibbings, the Fort Dunlop building was the largest factory in the world when it was completed and employed 3,200 under one roof. The Dunlop Tyre Company itself was founded in 1901 to make tyres for bicycles, most of which would have been built in Birmingham and Coventry. Dunlop became one of Birmingham's largest employers, helped along by its facilities that included a pub, theatre and playing fields.

Above: Due to fierce competition from foreign tyre producers the company went out of business and was sold in the 1980s. Fort Dunlop lay empty and derelict for 20 years without a commercial buyer. In 1999 it was bought by property developer Urban Splash who successfully converted it, starting in 2004 with top grade offices. The shell of the building was retained but the striking blue slab of wall at the far end of the building (see inset) is part of a new Travelodge hotel extension. The designers opened up the interior of the old factory with a new atrium and turned the arid asphalt roof into a green roof. Today it is occupied by a wide variety of new businesses, including the Birmingham Post and Mail, who moved in from their city centre offices. It is highly visible and recognisable from the eastbound elevated section of the M6 motorway between junction 6, Spaghetti Junction, and Junction 5, Castle Bromwich.

CASTLE BROMWICH AERODROME / CASTLE VALE ESTATE

'Spitfire Island' is a reminder of the crucial role played by test pilots here during the Second World War

Left: Some 50 Spitfire fighter planes and three Lancaster bombers can be counted on the apron next to the runway of Castle Bromwich Aerodrome in this wartime photo. The Berwood Playing Fields were made into the aerodrome in 1914 and continued to be used for that purpose until 1960 when it was closed due to the expansion of Elmdon Airport. The airfield was used to test the military aircraft that were built in the factory on the other side of the Chester Road and in 1920 the site was used for the British Industries Fair, the forerunner of Bingley Hall and the National Exhibition Centre. The finished aircraft were towed across the road to the aerodrome for their test flights. Winston Churchill is pictured inset with chief Spitfire test pilot Alex Henshaw at Castle Bromwich Aerodrome in 1941.

Above: After the airfield closed the site was sold for housing. City Council started to build the Castle Vale council housing estate in 1964, using the main runways for the three main roads. Some streets and tower blocks carry names that recall the area's history and the part it played in the Second World War. During the 1980s the estate was seen as a place of high social deprivation but following the formation of the Castle Vale Housing Trust in 1993 to take over the management of the estate, the area has seen a dramatic improvement. This was recognised by the Birmingham Civic Society when it awarded the Trust its 2002 Forward Prize. The 16m (52ft) high *Sentinel* sculpture in the photo was designed by Tim Tolkien and unveiled in 2000 by Alex Henshaw. It stands on a traffic island known locally as Spitfire Island at the junction of Chester Road and the A47 Fort Parkway, beyond which stands one of the tower blocks on the Castle Vale Estate.

GREEN LANE BATHS AND LIBRARY / GREEN LANE MOSQUE

Saved from dereliction by its current owners

Left: The firm of Martin and Chamberlain designed so many terracotta public buildings in Birmingham in the 19th century that the work of another architect, Henry Martin, was assumed even by Pevsner and Bryan Little to be the work of William Martin (1829–1900). But the architect of this building was Henry Martin who ran his own practice from an office in the city centre from 1892 to 1901. He was born around 1850 and died some time after 1914. His only major work was this Public Library and Baths at Green Lane, Small Heath, which opened in two phases in 1893 and 1902. It was surrounded by streets of terrace houses with no bathrooms and only murky canals or shallow streams in which the people of Small Heath could swim.

Right: In 1977 the buildings were vacated by the City Council and left to the mercy of the elements. Today it is Grade II listed and houses the Green Lane Mosque, officially the Markazi Jamiat Ahl-e-Hadith. Gradually the entire complex has been brought back into use with the mosque's own money and small amounts of public funding to restore the clock tower and provide living accommodation for teachers. The government's Community Programme helped convert the First Class baths in the 1980s. The library became the administrative centre, the Second Class baths were filled in and converted to a community hall. The slipper baths were taken out and the space integrated in the mosque. Recently the boiler house was converted to student flats and its windows replaced by custom-built, double-glazed units that matched the originals. The chimney is listed separately as a reminder of the boiler's coal-fired past. The owners have rescued it from dereliction and given it a new lease of life. The building is currently being re-roofed and re-glazed, while the terracotta and red brickwork is being cleaned to remove a hundred years' worth of grime.

BSA / GOLDEN HILLOCK ROAD

In its heyday BSA employed 28,000 people over 67 factories

Left: BSA (Birmingham Small Arms) workers hurry home in this 1953 photograph when the factory in Small Heath was busy making motorcycles. Before 1860, guns, for which Birmingham was famous, were made in small workshops in the city centre, but due to the demands of war BSA was formed and built a new factory in Small Heath, alongside the Grand Union Canal and close to the new station on the Oxford railway line. Workers houses were built next to the factory in Armoury Road so that they could easily walk to work every day. The multi-storey, concrete-framed factory in the photo was constructed in 1915 to manufacture armaments. The design of this Truscon (Trussed Concrete Steel Company) building was remarkable for its time. It was the earliest example of a Truscon or reinforced-concrete building in the UK. Motorcycles were tested on a steep mound in the grounds known locally as 'the Ackers' because the canal crosses the River Cole here on an aqueduct.

Above: In 1971 workers at the BSA factory staged a demonstration under the banner 'Keep the BSA Going', but its collapse in 1972 marked the end of motor manufacturing in Small Heath. By 1973 the BSA workforce had been cut from 4,500 to 1,500 and the company was merged with Norton-Villiers. The factory was demolished in 1977 and only one part of it remains at the far end of the site. The rest has been redeveloped as an industrial estate and a mobile phone mast is prominent in the centre of the site. The test hill now has an artificial ski-slope and a rock-face (opened by Chris Bonington) that is managed by the Ackers Trust, which was formed in 1983 and runs other adventure and canal-based activities on the site. The whole area is dense with new trees, some of which were planted by David Bellamy when he visited the project in the 1970s. Small Heath Station, which had served the BSA since it was opened in 1860, still exists today, although not all trains stop here any more. At its height, BSA employed 28,000 people over 67 factories, with 11,000 employees living in the Small Heath area. It was one of the first big companies to employ women and it pioneered free health and welfare for its employees.

ST ANDREW'S STADIUM

Home to Birmingham City Football Club since 1906

Left: The 'Blues' began life in 1875 as the Small Heath Alliance. The stadium – their second after moving from the Onion Trenches at Muntz Street in 1905 – was named after the parish and the nearby St Andrew's Church. At the beginning of the 20th century Small Heath was packed with terrace houses and floodlighting was only installed at the stadium in 1956. This aerial photo from 1968 shows the curve of the Coventry Road on the top right corner where it joins Cattell Road. Tilton Road defines the far end of the pitch and the Bristol and Birmingham railway line, crossed by the St Andrew's Road bridge, defines the other end. The ornate ventilation tower of St Andrew's School occupies the bottom right of the picture and to the left is the distinctive Dutch-style Holmes council housing estate on Garrison Lane.

Above: This photo shows the roofs of the new stands on three sides of the pitch. The Holmes council estate is on the left and St Andrew's School is in the right foreground. Beyond the stadium is a new superstore that looks almost as big as the Blues' pitch. After the 1993–94 season the Kop and the Tilton Road terraces were demolished and replaced with a new 7,000-seat Tilton Road Stand and a 9,500-seat Kop Stand. The Railway Stand was built in 1999 and seats 8,000. It was renamed in 2009 to honour Gil Merrick who was considered one of the best goalkeepers in the country during the mid 1950s and who spent his entire career with the Blues. Although Birmingham City has continued to play at top level, it has not been as successful as its old rival Aston Villa. The Blues have never won the FA Cup. Karren Brady, then only 23 years old, became the club's managing director in 1992. She left in 2009 and is now vice chairman of West Ham United.

CANNON HILL PARK

This popular park includes areas for boating, fishing, bowls, tennis and putting

Left: The 57-acre Cannon Hill Park and the boating pool seen in this picture were opened to the public in 1873. Louisa Ryland, the wealthy landowner who donated the park to the Corporation wanted no ceremony to mark the occasion nor did she want the park named in her honour. By the time this photo was taken around 1910 the many varieties of trees that were planted had matured to make the park a haven of green and peace in the middle of the still-growing industrial city.

Above: A boathouse and landing stage have appeared since the c. 1910 photo. On the left is a terrace of artists' studios built in the 1960s, a romantic notion that appears not to have been a success as they are now used for other purposes. Just beyond, and out of sight here, is a working scale model of the Corporation's Elan Valley Reservoir in mid-Wales, where Birmingham gets its water supply. Otherwise the scene is the same and peopled likewise with children feeding ducks as it was a hundred years earlier. Cannon Hill is the city's most popular public park. Not only does it offer all the amenities of the classic urban park, it is also the home of the Midlands Arts Centre and the location of the Golden Lion Inn, a medieval timber-framed building that was moved here from Deritend in 1911.

MOSELEY VILLAGE

The 16th-century St Mary's Church and the Bull's Head inn still dominate this view

Left: The church and tower of St Mary's Church, which has stood here since the early 16th century, and the old Bull's Head dominate this 1873 photograph of Moseley Village Green. George Clements was listed as the landlord of the inn at this time with J. Elliott, Florist, next door. We are looking east across the Alcester Road to Wake Green Road. Salisbury Road – which is behind the camera in the present-day photo, and which was named after Conservative Prime Minister Lord Salisbury – was not cut until 1896. Moseley had a railway station of its own, opened in 1867 on the Gloucester line. This no doubt helped Moseley to grow rapidly in the late 19th century.

Above: The rebuilt pub is still called the Bull's Head and St Mary's Church is much the same except that it has a set of solar panels on its roof that are partially visible from the street. In 1983 the church and its grounds were incorporated in the Moseley Conservation Area. The Green is the hub of the Moseley Farmers' Market that takes place every fourth Saturday of the month from 9am to 3pm, with over 50 stallholders from farms and other centres of food production. It won a FARMA (National Farmers' Retail Markets Association) award as the best farmers' market of 2009 and 2012. The award is made to markets that exemplify a passion for local food, a commitment to farming and the environment and a talent for retail. Any profits made from organising the market are put back into the community via a not-for-profit company. Moseley lost its station in 1941 but it may come back if a new rail link can be made to Moor Street Station at Camp Hill.

EDGBASTON CRICKET GROUND

The UK's second-largest cricketing venue after Lord's Cricket Ground in London

Left: The distinctive Thwaite Memorial Scoreboard built in 1950 is at the centre of this view of the famous Edgbaston cricket ground. The committee of the Warwickshire County Cricket Club decided on Edgbaston rather than Rugby or Leamington Spa because of its good railway connections. Flood-prone land alongside the River Rea was leased from Lord Calthorpe and the first match was held here in 1886 against the MCC. In this 1955 photo the ground staff are testing a new machine that sucks up water from the pitch watched by various officials. The weather is of course an important element in the English game of cricket but the spectators were clearly expected to sit in the open stand to the right of the scoreboard and bring umbrellas for the occasional shower. The landmark spire in the background belongs to the red terracotta church of St Mary and St Ambrose that stands on the corner of Raglan Road and Pershore Road beyond the northern boundary of the stadium.

Above: After its £32 million redevelopment Edgbaston can now seat 25,000 spectators in its comfortable new stands bordering Edgbaston Road. This makes it the second only to Lord's in size. To orientate the view, the spire of St Mary and St Ambrose in the 1955 photo can still be seen to the left of the new main entrance. Floodlighting masts now soar over the four corners of the pitch to allow evening matches but what can't be controlled is the English weather. Tradition has it that cricket stadia, unlike the new Wimbledon and Wembley ones, are never protected entirely from the rain. The turf-drying machine from the 1955 photo mustn't have proved successful. In 1981 Edgbaston started to use a large pitch covering that became known as the Brumbrella. The flat rainproof cover was quick to roll out but was deemed to have an adverse effect on the pitch, which led to its eventual removal in 2000.

BIRMINGHAM UNIVERSITY

Chamberlain Tower is the tallest freestanding clock tower in the world

Left: The buildings and Tuscan-style campanile designed by Aston Webb and Ingress Bell form the heart of the University of Birmingham. The buildings shown here in 1939 were laid out in Beaux Arts style between 1900 and 1909. Perhaps the architects were inspired by the idea that Birmingham had more miles of canal within its boundary than Venice. The new campus for what began life as Mason College in 1880 was due to two benefactors – Lord Calthorpe who donated 25 acres of land on his family estate, and Andrew Carnegie who offered £50,000 to establish a first-class modern scientific college on the new site. The chapel-like building is the Great Hall and beyond it is the slender 100m (328ft) tall Joseph Chamberlain Memorial Clock Tower. The tower, known as 'Old Joe', was designed to stand at the centre of the university's semicircle of matching red brick buildings.

Above: The mature trees now block the modern summertime view of all but the tips of the original buildings, while hard-wearing, maintenance-free artificial turf has replaced grass for the sports pitches nearby. It took a hundred years to fill the final gap in the planned redbrick semicircle. The most recent addition is the £16 million Bramell Music Building and 450-seat concert hall, the top of which was only craned into place in March 2012. Rather than design something in the style of 2012, the architect, Glenn Howells, has replicated the original 1900 style so that it is virtually impossible to tell the difference between old and new. After the Second World War, government funding enabled the university to expand rapidly to a development plan devised by Casson and Conder in 1957. Various faculty buildings have been designed by different modernist architects. Andy Foster notes in the 2005 Pevsner guide that as a concentrated experience of 1960s university architecture Birmingham remains hard to beat.

QUEEN ELIZABETH HOSPITAL
All services have now transferred to the new Queen Elizabeth Hospital Birmingham

Left: This huge complex was designed by Lanchester and Lodge between 1933 and 1938 with several later additions by the same architects. This picture shows it soon after completion when there were still remnants of farmland around. The single-storey flat-roofed buildings on the right look more like building contractors' huts than permanent hospital buildings. The new roads were free of traffic and quiet enough for the two women to stroll deep in conversation along Hospital Drive. The university's Chamberlain Tower on the right of the hospital, beyond the projecting south-facing balconies, shows that this view is to the south-east.

Above: The location of the old photo is now occupied by the Women's Hospital, but a similar if more distant view can be gained from the boundary of the sports ground on Metchley Lane. The very top of the university's Chamberlain Tower can now be seen to the left of the hospital clock tower. The original suite of buildings has remained remarkably intact, perhaps due to the quality of its construction and the classic dignity of its architecture, despite the completion of the new Queen Elizabeth Hospital Birmingham close to this site in 2010–11. All remaining services had transferred to the new hospital by October 2011. It has been said that demolishing the old hospital would be very costly so it seems that the building with its distinctive clock tower may be with us for some time to come. The new Selly Oak Bypass has also opened up a panoramic view of the two hospitals side-by-side (not shown from this angle), as if to give the observer of architecture a convenient opportunity of comparing their contrasting styles.

BOURNVILLE

Cadbury has been making chocolate from this site since 1879

Left: These are the first houses built by Richard and George Cadbury in 1879 for their key workers next to their new chocolate factory at Bournbrook Hall, four miles from their first premises in the centre of Birmingham. Cadbury at first built 143 homes and sold them to workers at cost price. By 1893 Cadbury owned 120 acres of land close to the works and by 1900 it included 313 cottages and houses. The first houses were typical of the large Victorian villas being built at the time. Each house occupied only a quarter of the land allotted to it – the rest was kept for gardens. The estate was built and managed by the newly created Bournville Village Trust. The factory (shown on the left and in the foreground) was next to the canal and was connected to the nearby railway line by a loop to carry Cadbury's own coal wagons.

Above: The original houses were demolished in the 1920s to make way for Bournville Place, the factory's four-storey dining hall. The building was remodelled for Cadbury Trebor Bassett in 2005 by Stanton Williams who converted it into office space for up to 700 people. The green in front of the building is used by Bournville Cricket Club. The building on the right is the Cadbury Cricket Pavilion. Also known as the Coronation Cricket Pavilion, it opened in 1902 to commemorate the coronation of King Edward VII. Although Cadbury was sold to Kraft Foods in 2010, so far the Bournville factory and its workforce appear to be secure. According to a recent Birmingham Post report each year the factory produces around 15 million tins of Roses chocolates, more than 45 million Easter eggs and around 300 million Creme Eggs. Every 24 hours, almost 17 million Dairy Milk Buttons, now with a Fair Trade mark, come off the production line. The popular Cadbury World visitor centre is on the factory estate.

SYCAMORE ROAD, BOURNVILLE

This view remains virtually unchanged thanks to the Bournville Village Trust

Left: Traffic and people are sparse in this c. 1910 photograph of the newly built shops at 35–47 Sycamore Road in the heart of Bournville village. The shops were designed by H. Bedford Taylor and completed in 1908 opposite Bournville Green. The spaciousness of the layout and the traditional style of the buildings were in contrast to the densely packed 'by-law' housing that was surrounding the old city centre in areas such as Sparkbrook, Balsall Heath, Handsworth, Small Heath, Duddeston and Aston. This was due to the ideas of the Quaker chocolate manufacturer, George Cadbury, who moved his business from the city centre for better hygiene and public health. He also wanted to be close to canal and rail transport for bringing in the milk, sugar and cocoa and delivering the finished products.

Above: Thanks to the insight of its founder in forming the Bournville Village Trust, whose Estate Office is in this row of shops, the appearance of the buildings and the quality of the surrounding landscape has been maintained as intended. The Rest House (inset) was built on the Green in 1914 and the road which originally bounded the northern side of the triangular shaped Green has been turned into a footpath. The road bounding its western side was renamed Linden Road up to where it becomes Oak Tree Lane on its way north to Selly Oak.

BOURNVILLE BATHS
Built for Cadbury's factory workers

Left: The indoor Swimming Baths on Bournville Lane and the Friends' Meeting House on Bournville Green were the first buildings planned by George Cadbury to cater for both the physical and spiritual health of his factory workers. The baths, which were designed by G. H. Lewin and opened in 1904, were described by Pevsner in 1966 as 'the most impressive architectural extravaganza of the whole estate'. This seems surprising as Quakers were known for their austerity and the simplicity of their homes and meeting houses. There is a decorative Arts and Crafts style panel by Benjamin Creswick on the front gable. It depicts two trees with the date and name of the baths carved in stone. The women in this 1909 photo look like factory or office workers hurrying home. They may also be heading for a session in the baths, which was for women only. Just past the baths can be seen one of the first Bournville houses built by Cadbury in 1879.

Right: The exterior of the building looks unchanged but it is many years since it was used as a swimming baths and no other use seems to have been found for it. Mature forest trees now partially obscure the modern view of the baths. To the right, plain modernist buildings contrast with the baths' multi-gabled side elevation. On the left, a 1920s brick-built administration block stands on the site of the first Bournville houses built in 1879. On the side wall of the baths, a brass plaque below the 1879 datestone (inset) reads: 'In front of this stone stood the house built in 1879 for William Tallis the first Works Foreman after Richard and George Cadbury transferred their business to Bournville. The stone was taken from the house on its demolition in 1967.'

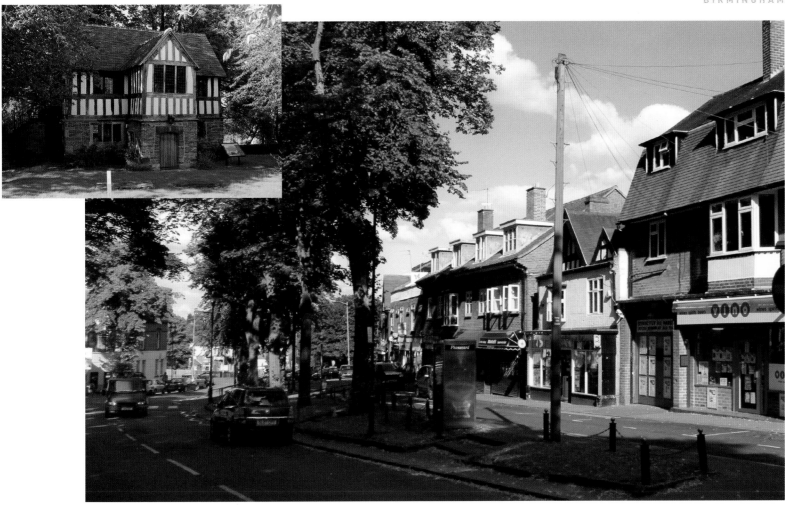

KINGS NORTON
Site of an annual Mop Fair since 1616

Left: The Green at Kings Norton, shown here in 1963, has been the scene of the two-day annual Mop Fair on Old Michaelmas Day (10 October) since 1616. These fairs, which still take place in many old market towns such as Alcester, Evesham, Stratford-upon-Avon and Warwick, began as hiring fairs, when people looking for work paraded in their Sunday best wearing a badge of their trade. Servants and domestic workers that didn't have a particular trade carried a mop head or wore a tassel on their lapels. Once they had been hired they could enjoy the fun of the fair. The twin half-timbered gables over the white building on the right indicate that this is oldest building in the picture. Nearby but out of the picture is the Old Grammar School (inset above). This ancient two-storey building sitting in the peaceful graveyard of Kings Norton Church was once a place of learning. According to Pevsner, the original 15th-century building was the priest's house. It is thought to have been used as a library by Thomas Hall, a puritanical Protestant, in the 17th century, before being used as a school until 1878.

Above: The red GPO telephone kiosk has been replaced with a British Telecom phone box and the ownership of the shops and their shop fronts has changed. Otherwise, the row of buildings in this scene is much the same. Enthusiasts of the Old Grammar School (inset) won a competition in 2004 for a grant of £2.5 million from the Heritage Lottery Fund to restore the building. The restoration of the building was not intended to return it to its original condition but to respect the many alterations that had been made over the centuries. For example, it is thought that the ground floor was originally open to the elements and the upper story supported on a timber frame. The fireplaces and chimney shafts are recent additions and the open external staircase was only added in 1910. By looking at the building we can trace its history and see how its owners have adapted it to meet different needs at different periods of its long life. The Grade II listed building is currently used for small meetings.

LICKEY HILLS
The hills were designated a Country Park in 1971

Left: Day trippers from the densely built-up suburbs of Birmingham would arrive here at the Rednal terminus on the number 70 tram. They would be rewarded with a bracing ramble up one of the Lickey Hills – Bilberry Hill, seen in the background, Rednal Hill or Beacon Hill. On the left is a cast-iron Corporation Transport clock and on the right the terminus building where the drivers and conductors took their refreshment and rest before starting back to the city centre. The Roman road from Metchley Fort arrived at Rednal then climbed over the Lickey Hills, through the dip between Bilberry Hill and Beacon Hill, before descending to Droitwich (Salinae) and Worcester. The author of *Lord of the Rings*, J. R. R Tolkien lived in Rednal in 1904 and must have tramped the hills as a youngster.

Above: The last tram ran in 1953 but the tramlines and granite setts are still there beside the terminus building, which is now a Chinese restaurant. The Lickey Hills Country Park was designated in 1971 and is run by Worcestershire County Council because it lies entirely outside the Birmingham boundary. The Park attracts 500,000 visitors a year but they mostly arrive by car and park in one of three car parks: one serves the Visitor Centre that was opened in 1990 near the top of Bilberry Hill; one serves the Rose Hill Hotel and the Golf Club at the bottom of the hill; and another is on the summit of Beacon Hill, where there is a direction indicator on a small castle-like structure and a splendid view of the Malvern Hills to the south.

LONGBRIDGE MOTOR WORKS
Once one of the biggest automobile works in Europe

Left: The history of the Longbridge Works is littered with success and failure, controversy and conflict, but in its heyday it employed thousands on its production lines. When Pevsner was writing his guide in 1966 he described Longbridge as the centre of the Austin Morris Division of the British Leyland Motor Corporation. He wrote, 'The first factory rose on a small site here in 1905 and grew rapidly into one of the biggest automobile works in Europe.' Particularly impressive was the Car Assembly Hangar designed by one of America's foremost industrial architects, Howard Crane. This 1939 photo was taken when trams still ran on Lickey Road to and from the Rednal terminus. Lord Austin ran his Motor Company from an office in the building on the right of the photo, next to 'K' Gate.

Above: Austin joined Morris to become the British Motor Corporation but by 1968 it became British Leyland. The nationalised company was made famous in the late 1970s by the disruptive activities of trade unionist 'Red Robbo', but despite this a new model, the Austin Metro, began to be produced at Longbridge in 1980. MG Rover was wound up in 2006 and bought by Nangjing. The Chinese company now makes a relatively small number of MG Rover cars at Longbridge. Demolition of most of the factory began soon after and the last to face the bulldozer was the historic South Works where the company started. Demolition of the Car Assembly Hangar began towards the end of 2011. In place of the South Works a shiny new Bournville College (the white wedge-shaped building) has been built to replace the campus in Bournville and plans have been published for the rebuilding of what will be a new town on the rubble of the Longbridge Works.

BOTANICAL GARDENS

The completed gardens were opened to members of the Birmingham Botanical and Horticultural Society in 1832

Left: The 15-acre gardens in Edgbaston were designed by J. C. Loudon in 1829 on land leased from the prosperous Lord Calthorpe's Estate. The 1884 Terrace Glasshouses are by Henry Hope, a famous Smethwick company that specialised in metal window frames, including those for the Houses of Parliament. The completed gardens were opened to subscribers in 1832 but in 1851 it was decided to open them on Mondays to 'working class' people at a penny per head admission. The *Morning Chronicle* reported that within two years nearly 50,000 Monday 'perambulators' a year were coming in and that, 'if summer had not come to an end the lawn certainly should'. The pressure must have eased when public parks like Cannon Hill Park, opened in 1873, began to appear around the city amongst the rows of workers' housing.

Above: The chimney and the oldest greenhouses are still recognisable, but the white building on the right is now a restaurant, which hosted Bill Clinton and Tony Blair during the 1998 G8 Summit in Birmingham. The Botanical Gardens has kept most of its original features, which include Tropical, Subtropical, Mediterranean and Arid glasshouses, a bandstand and various aviaries, one of which has housed the talkative Jenny, a Sulphur-crested Cockatoo, for the last 30 years. Recent additions are the British National Bonsai Collection and an art gallery. Within easy reach of housing estates, business premises and private schools, the lawn is well-used by parents and young children on sunny days, just as it was in the 1950s photograph.

EDGBASTON RESERVOIR

The reservoir has been topping up Birmingham's canal system since 1827

Left: Rotton Park Reservoir, otherwise known as Edgbaston Reservoir, was built in 1827 by Thomas Telford, not for drinking water but to gather water from local streams to top up the canal system. Lying on high ground just below the ridge occupied by Birmingham city centre, and on the eastern or Trent side of the English Watershed, its water could end up on either side of it via the canal system. Birmingham lacks a major river of its own, but Telford's reservoir provided a golden opportunity for water sports to flourish. The Birmingham Rowing Club was established in 1873 and serious rowing is thriving in this 1950s photograph.

Above: The boatshed of the Birmingham Rowing Club is at the far end of the public car park with the entrance from Reservoir Road. Although not the spectator sport it seems to have been in the 1950s, club and college rowers can be seen launching their boats here provided the water level is high enough. In the drought conditions of early 2012 Severn Trent Water pumped in enough water from the canal to raise the level to its maximum. A local voluntary organisation, Friends of Edgbaston Reservoir, helps the council wardens to look after the shore-side paths, landscape and resident wildlife. The circuit of the reservoir, including the crossing of the top of the dam, has become popular with walkers, joggers, and cyclists.

SOHO ROAD

Home to a convent, mosque and Buddhist temple, this is one of the most religiously diverse roads in Britain

Left: The Soho Road, part of Thomas Telford's highway from Birmingham to Holyhead, is taken over by a parade of cyclists to mark the coronation of Edward VII in this photo from August 1902. Edward was the first monarch from the House of Saxe Coburg and Gotha, but his son George V who succeeded him in 1910, diplomatically renamed it the House of Windsor. Since the Safety Bicycle was invented a decade earlier, with a chain drive to the rear wheel and pneumatic tyres invented by Dunlop in Birmingham, cycling had become very popular and local clubs organised tours and races for their members. The Handsworth Free library, the clock tower of which can be seen in the distance, was opened in 1880 to satisfy the growing demand for books and newspapers. In 1902 Handsworth was an independent district in the County of Staffordshire.

Above: Many of the shops, including the library clock tower, appear much the same, but the tramlines are gone. Now cars, buses and heavy goods vehicles jostle for road space. The district of Handsworth was taken over by Birmingham Corporation in 1911 and is now firmly within the boundary of Birmingham City Council. No longer a trunk road to Holyhead after the construction of the M6 and M54 motorways, the Soho Road is a thriving shopping street. It is at the heart of the diverse Handsworth community whose members made it their home after the Second World War and the end of an Empire that King Edward VII ruled. Each April the Soho Road is thronged with hundreds of orange-clothed Sikhs holding their Vaisakhi procession in honour of their founder. The ornate dome that can be seen at the far end belongs to a Sikh temple, the Soho Road Gurdwara. Handsworth Library is still serving the local community and now includes books and newspapers in Punjabi, Urdu, Gujerati and Bengali.

ROTUNDA VIEW
A panoramic view over the north-west of Birmingham

Left: The 24-storey Rotunda was designed by Birmingham architect James Roberts as part of the 1960s Bullring development. It was opened as an office block in 1965 and soon became a well-known landmark because of its unique shape. This 1966 view from the Rotunda is north-west to the unfinished Post Office Tower, which dwarfs the dome of St Philip's Cathedral and the more distant slender spire of St Paul's Church (both on the right). To the right of the cathedral, is the aptly named Grand Hotel. This French Renaissance style building, bounded by Colmore Row, Church Street, Barwick Street and Livery Street, was designed by Thomson Plevins and opened in 1879. The big neon sign in the lower right-hand corner belongs to ABC Television in New Street, which started to broadcast weekend programmes in the Midlands in 1956.

Above: In 1997 the owners of the Rotunda intended to demolish it as part of the redevelopment of the 1960s Bullring, but in response to public demand it was decided to retain it instead. Urban Splash hired architect Glenn Howells to re-clad the entire building in floor-to-ceiling windows and convert the interior to luxury apartments. The view today is from the gallery on the top floor that provides a balcony for each penthouse apartment. In this view the Post Office, or Telecom Tower as it is now known, is bristling with microwave transmitters. To the left of the tower is the vacant NatWest office tower in Colmore Row. The canyon of New Street, at its junction with Corporation Street, is just visible in the lower left-hand corner. The inverted green ziggurat facades on the far right belong to One Snow Hill. The Grand Hotel, which is currently covered by scaffolding, closed in 2002 but there are plans to reopen it as a luxury 152-bedroom hotel in 2014. The end of the office block (City Centre House), on which the ABC sign was mounted, still has the old metal framework attached to it.